Growing in Jesus

BOOK ONE

Growing in Jesus

A resource for
families and young people

BOOK ONE

Barry Jackson

Growing in Jesus
A resource for families and young people
Published by Barry Jackson
with Castle Publishing Ltd
New Zealand

© 2024 Barry Jackson

ISBN 978-0-473-72272-2

Editing:
Rachel Ross

Production & Typesetting:
Andrew Killick
Castle Publishing Services
www.castlepublishing.co.nz

Cover Design & Illustration:
Paul Smith

All Scripture quotations, unless otherwise indicated, are taken from
the Holy Bible, New Living Translation,
Copyright © 1996, 2004, 2015 by Tyndale House Foundation.
Used by permission of Tyndale House Publishers, Inc.,
Carol Stream, Illinois 60188.
All rights reserved.

ALL RIGHTS RESERVED

No part of this publication may be reproduced,
stored in a retrieval system, or transmitted
in any form or by any means, electronic, mechanical,
photocopying, recording or otherwise,
without prior written permission from the author.

For more, visit www.growinginjesus.nz

I am writing to you who are God's children
because your sins have been forgiven through Jesus.

1 John 2:12

And now, just as you accepted Christ Jesus as your Lord,
you must continue to follow him. Let your roots grow down into him,
and let your lives be built on him. Then your faith will grow strong in
the truth you were taught, and you will overflow with thankfulness.

Colossians 2:6-7

Contents

Acknowledgements	9
Preface	11
Introduction	15
How to use Growing in Jesus	19
Week 1: What things are wonderful to you?	25
Week 2: What is God like? Part 1	29
Week 3: What is God like? Part 2	33
Week 4: What is God like? Part 3	37
Week 5: What did God do in creation?	41
Week 6: How did God create humans?	45
Week 7: What is God's will for us?	49
Week 8: Where do we find God's will?	53
Week 9: Who is Jesus?	57
Week 10: What are angels and what do they do?	62
Week 11: How does God watch over our lives?	66
Week 12: What does it mean that God has a plan for my life?	70
Week 13: What happened when Adam and Eve were tempted to do wrong?	74
Week 14: What is sin?	78
Week 15: How have humans and creation been damaged by sin?	82
Week 16: What remedy did God provide for Adam and Eve's sin?	87
Week 17: What does God's grace mean?	91
Week 18: Why did the Lord Jesus need to become human?	95
Week 19: What is the love of God like?	100
Week 20: Why did God have to give his Son for us?	104
Week 21: What does it mean for us to believe?	108
Week 22: What is eternal life and when does it start?	112
Week 23: What did Jesus mean when he talked about repentance?	117
Week 24: What happened when the Lord Jesus rose from the dead?	122

Week 25: What is powerful about the Cross?	128
Week 26: What is special about Christian fellowship?	132
Week 27: Where is the Lord Jesus now, and what is heaven like?	136
Week 28: How do we grow as Jesus' followers?	140
Week 29: What does God say about how valuable we are?	144
Week 30: What will happen at the end of time when Jesus returns?	148
Week 31: What did Jesus mean when he talked about the world?	153
Week 32: What is the special meaning of being in God's family, the church?	158
Week 33: Why do we still do the wrong thing sometimes?	162
Week 34: How do we grow in our relationship with God?	166
Week 35: How do we become more like the Lord Jesus?	171
Week 36: What does the Bible teach us about temptation?	175
Week 37: What does it mean to be filled with God's Spirit?	179
Week 38: What does hope mean for a Christian?	183
Week 39: What does it mean when we say the Bible is inspired by the Holy Spirit?	187
Week 40: What does the Bible say about God's promises to us?	191
Week 41: What do the Ten Commandments teach us about our relationship with God?	195
Week 42: How do the Ten Commandments help us to get along well with each other? Part 1	200
Week 43: How do the Ten Commandments help us to get along well with each other? Part 2	205
Week 44: What does holy communion mean?	210
Week 45: What is baptism about?	214
Week 46: How does the Lord carry our burdens?	218
Week 47: How are we to pray?	222
Week 48: What does worship mean?	227
Week 49: How does God want us to give to help others?	231
Week 50: What did God do at Christmas?	235
Week 51: What does it mean to have God as our Father?	239
Week 52: How do I set a good foundation for my life?	243

Acknowledgements

I would like to thank my good friend Ian Smith for his support and encouragement in the early stages of this project. Craig McDonald and his Year 7 class at Cornerstone Christian School provided great feedback and encouragement in trialling the first draft of *Growing in Jesus*. Families at Palmerston North Central Baptist have generously given it a real-life test and have given valuable practical feedback. I am grateful to Andrew at Castle Publishing who has been a superb guide, listener and highly professional guiding hand in the production process. Finally, but most of all, my grateful thanks goes to my wonderful wife of 40 years, Linda, who has been unwaveringly supportive from the start of this project.

Preface

Providing a framework for our children's spiritual growth and praying for them are our most important roles as parents. Although it is ultimately their choice whether they commit their lives to Christ, the seeds of the Good News that we sow into their lives have potential for eternity as well as for good in this life.

Many years ago, as young parents, we had great difficulty finding resources to raise our children spiritually. We never had a training course for parenting, and it is likely that you haven't either. We read a bible story with them at bedtime each night from a series of children's bibles, prayed with them and referred to Scripture when helping them to decide what was right. We also tried, not very successfully, to read devotional stories together at mealtimes when they were a little older. There was little available in terms of devotional or teaching resources that seemed helpful.

As a teacher, and particularly from that part of my career working in Christian schools, my perception, which is widely shared among Christian educators and leaders, is that there is a decline in biblical literacy among young people in these days. This lack of a biblical foundation leads to struggles among young people in knowing how to live fulfilled lives that glorify the Lord Jesus in a rapidly changing world. *Growing in Jesus* is written as a guide to historic and widely held Christian beliefs and practices.

Growing in Jesus is written at a reading level to suit young people from intermediate or middle school age. If you have younger children who would also like to join in, there are also questions written for them, along with practical activities.

Growing in Jesus is intended to be realistic and not burdensome on parents, so it is designed to be used with one topic over one to two nights per week. Each week, the topic includes two sets of questions structured for different ages and a practical activity. A single theme for each week sets us up for success in working through the resource rather than feelings of guilt if we miss a night or two.

The primary theme and purpose of *Growing in Jesus* is choosing to follow Jesus and growing in faith in him. *Growing in Jesus* is written to point to the Lord Jesus Christ. Its aim is spiritual transformation not religious information.

Growing in Jesus is not written as a parenting guide, although any sincere time spent in God's Word and responding to it will make us better people and better parents. Other people have written parenting guides much better than I could attempt! Along the way, matters of Christian values and ethics will also arise and provide worthwhile discussion points as your children journey through life with you.

A final note to parents and young people

My denominational background in different places has been Methodist, Baptist, Anglican, Pentecostal and Baptist again. In writing, I have tried to avoid areas where there might be major theological differences and to instead focus on what unites us. We are all God's unfinished handiwork, so I know that I won't have managed it perfectly! Our shared life and love in the Lord Jesus Christ are our most precious gifts together.

Growing in Jesus has been planned as a resource to be used in families or classrooms. If you are a young person reading it by yourself or if you find anything confronting or confusing, please talk with a trusted adult, e.g. a pastor, youth leader or Christian teacher. You are loved, cared for and accepted by Jesus Christ with a love greater than any of us could imagine. He is with you, wanting to be your Friend.

For all of us there are things in life that we find hard – different things for each one of us and some things in common for all of us. I've been no exception and there are still things that I find hard today after 50 years as a Christian. Reading some of the stories and ideas in *Growing in Jesus* may bring some challenges to mind for you.

Preface

Please remember two things from John 3:17. It reads: 'God sent his Son into the world not to judge the world, but to save the world through him.' Firstly, God unconditionally loves, welcomes and accepts us because of Jesus. Secondly, Jesus is with us in the challenges we face and can bring us through them. We will find our wellbeing in Jesus as we walk with him step by step and trust him.

Growing in Jesus has been written out of a sense of call from God and 50 years after setting out to follow Jesus. This book is probably imperfect, but may God use it to help give young lives the rich experience of a growing relationship with him.

Introduction

We understand from Scripture that each person is deeply loved by God our Heavenly Father and that children are especially precious to him. In Mark 10:13-16, we read that Jesus welcomed children when others pushed them away, spoke of their trust in God, and held them in his arms and blessed them personally. Wonderfully, as we read in Psalm 139, God has already written in his own book his purpose for each day of our children's lives and invites both us and them to discover that purpose as we walk with him together.

Psalm 139:16 tells us:

> You saw me before I was born. Every day of my life was recorded in your book. Every moment was laid out before a single day had passed.

This story in God's book for each of our children includes every area of their lives – their personalities, giftings and future occupations, relationships and so on. Most importantly, on those pages are the circumstances and words that will lead them to encounter and hopefully to follow Jesus for themselves.

While we are raising our children, we don't usually get to see more than a glimpse of God's eternal future for them because we are head-down, tail-up in the busy craft of parenting, but as we share with God in helping write his book for our children, we have the Bible to guide us. A word of caution may be timely here. The Bible can't be used like a recipe for crispy skinned salmon or a set of instructions for assembling a flat pack desk. For us to have a real impact on our children's spiritual development as we share with them, the words of Scripture need to do their work in our lives first. The English evangelist Leonard Ravenhill said (slightly paraphrased):

> Words born in the head reach the head; words born in the heart reach the heart.

That is the power of example! Another way of putting it is that God's Word must do its work in conquering the self-life in us first before it can work through us. Our children will always imitate what we do before they follow what we say. Your love for God and his ways lived out in everyday life will be the greatest testimony to your children.

In the West, we live now in a world where having faith in Christ and living as his followers has ceased to be mainstream and, at times, is being opposed. This is seen in a continuing decline of biblically based moral and ethical values and in philosophies that are strongly human-centred and where each person develops their own 'truth'. Answers to life questions are, therefore, 'in here' rather than 'out there', where they have been revealed to us in God's Word. God's Word remains fully relevant even in this changing world, as 1 Peter 1:25b tells us:

> But the word of the Lord remains forever.

In Colossians 1:17b, we read that in speaking of the Lord Jesus: 'he holds all creation together.' In a world where we hear so many different messages, Jesus stands as the only one who provides answers that can be relied on both for this life and the next. Further, in Colossians 2:8-10, the Apostle Paul said:

> Don't let anyone capture you with empty philosophies and high-sounding nonsense that come from human thinking and from the spiritual powers of this world, rather than from Christ. For in Christ lives all the fullness of God in a human body. So, you also are complete through your union with Christ, who is the head over every ruler and authority.

That is an astounding statement – that in Jesus, we and our children can be filled and made complete by the living God.

A well-understood and well-lived faith in Christ is the best gift that we can give our children. If the world is becoming a little darker, the light of Jesus shines out even brighter. *Growing in Jesus* is a resource that seeks to offer a foundation of reasoned Biblical truth that points to life in Jesus in each weekly reading. At the same time, *Growing in Jesus* is intended to be more than just a teaching resource but a pointer to experiencing abundant life in Jesus. In 2 Corinthians 3:6, Paul wrote:

> This is a covenant not of written laws, but of the Spirit. The old written covenant ends in death; but under the new covenant, the Spirit gives life.

Giving the 'right' answers to questions is not a substitute for a living relationship with God our Father through the Lord Jesus. As parents we also want to avoid making family devotion times into 'religion' or 'legalism', or in our enthusiasm, setting an impossible standard for our children.

Deuteronomy 6:4-9 tells us:

> Listen, O Israel! The Lord is our God, the Lord alone. And you must love the Lord your God with all your heart, all your soul, and all your strength. And you must commit yourselves wholeheartedly to these commands that I am giving you today. Repeat them again and again to your children. Talk about them when you are at home and when you are on the road, when you are going to bed and when you are getting up. Tie them to your hands and wear them on your forehead as reminders. Write them on the doorposts of your house and on your gates.

So regular family devotions and teachable moments that occur when we are out and about with our children are both important.

In Psalm 103:7, we read:

> He revealed his character to Moses and his deeds to the people of Israel.

The people of Israel only saw from a distance what God did through his miracles in the wilderness, whereas Moses and his successor, Joshua, made the time and effort to have a more intimate relationship with God by learning his character and his ways. It takes time and effort to reflect on and respond to questions like 'What is God like? How does he do things? How does he want me to live?' but it comes with the precious reward of his presence. It pleases God when we get together as families to talk together about him and to learn his ways – so much so that he even writes it down as we read in Malachi 3:16:

> Then those who feared the Lord spoke with each other, and the Lord listened to what they said. In his presence, a scroll of remembrance was written to record the names of those who feared him and always thought about the honour of his name.

How to use Growing in Jesus

1. Spiritual scrapbook and treasure box

Consider starting a spiritual scrapbook with each of your children as you begin *Growing in Jesus*, where they begin to record their own spiritual journey with God. These scrapbooks could include stories, photos, drawings, prayers from grandparents (perhaps recruit some God-Grandparents if your own parents are not still living), their questions about God and so on. Things made at family devotions or children's church could also go into a treasure box. It might be a fun family activity to decorate a scrapbook and create a treasure box from something like an old shoe box with your children.

2. When to use this resource

Block in time and turn devices off. A small whiteboard (about A3 size) will be useful from time to time for writing lists or sketching things. Our church provides these for groups of parents who use *Growing in Jesus* as part of a box of resources. As in our own walk with God, giving quality and high-priority time to family devotions is of first importance. If your children see you doing this, later in life they will know how to deal with competing pressures, like sport, study and work, for themselves. Busyness doesn't go away; its nature just changes! Bath and bedtime for infants transforms into sport and music practice and homework as they grow up.

Matthew 6:33 says:

> Seek the Kingdom of God above all else, and live righteously, and he will give you everything you need.

So, when we make time to put God first in our lives, we are promised that we will gain what is most important. When the busy and anxious Martha asked Jesus to tell her sister Mary, who was sitting at Jesus' feet, to come and help her, Jesus replied in Luke 10:42:

> There is only one thing worth being concerned about. Mary has discovered it, and it will not be taken away from her.

On the other hand, making spiritual development a priority in your family while avoiding making it an onerous or lifeless duty is vital. We want our children to get the message that keeping God's commands comes with the reward of his promises, so include games, fun, celebrations, and rewards. Ephesians 6:4 gives us advice about this practical balance:

> Fathers, do not provoke your children to anger by the way you treat them. Rather, bring them up with the discipline and instruction that comes from the Lord.

3. How *Growing in Jesus* is structured

Jim Hurn, a lecturer at Faith Bible College, once said in a lecture that Jesus started his ministry at a party (John 2:1-11) and finished with a picnic (John 21:9), so the word 'PARTY' is used as an acronym to approach each week's session.

> *P* repare and pray
> *A* sk
> *R* ead
> *T* est

Activit *Y*

Prepare and pray. Read over the topic for each week beforehand and give some thought to each block of questions. Consider adding stories from your own life to those I have included.

Prepare the equipment and materials needed for the activity. At the beginning of your family devotion, pray as a family, asking God to give meaning to your hearts and minds.

*A*sk your children what they already know or think using the open-ended question in the title of the weekly theme to begin some discussion.

*R*ead the topic for the week to your children.

*T*est their understanding with the questions at the end of the reading and find ways to answer any questions that come up.

Activit*Y*. Do the activity together as a family as time allows, chatting about how it relates to the theme of the weekly topic. A weekly approach you might use would be to go through the reading and ask the questions one day then do the practical activity on a second day.

4. Age of children

The weekly sessions are written at a level to be understood by 11- to 12-year-olds. If you have younger children you wish to include, you may need to paraphrase, or leave some topics until later, to suit their ages and needs. The Bible talks about people 'warts and all', so you may feel that some of the Scriptures, topics or examples would be best left until they are a bit older. You may also wish to have older children read or help lead the occasional session. If your children are still small you may wish to go through *Growing in Jesus* just using the activities and maybe the first block of questions. Later, you could perhaps go through it again when they are older, focusing on answering the discussion questions.

There's nothing wrong with passing on memories of family history either, especially if there are believers from way back. I am a first-generation Christian, but if I dig further into the past, I find there are some wonderful stories of people who have followed God. As our children get older, they especially like to hear these stories.

5. Questions and activities

Questions are provided in a variety of formats at the end of each weekly session and serve to check how well the ideas in the session have been understood. The first few questions, *To answer*, are at the level of younger children, while the last few questions, *To discuss*, are more open-ended and suitable for intermediate-aged children and teens. Copying the puzzle-type questions for younger children onto a mini whiteboard can make them easier to answer together. These activities will be available as a PDF to print out on www.growinginjesus.nz. The practical activities, *To do*, are planned to be broadly relevant to the weekly theme and are suitable for a dinner table or perhaps a kitchen bench. They suit more hands-on learning styles and are intended to add a fun element. Many of them have a science, craft or games approach.

6. Tricky bits

Scriptural truths are best taught from our hearts as well as our heads, so I encourage you to take time to prayerfully read through the devotional theme each week. Ask the Holy Spirit to guide you with a sense of what he is doing in your children's lives.

Encourage the asking of questions as well – that is how we learn. As we seek to foster a faith in our children, the Scriptures tell us that seeking after an ever-deepening faith in God is a lifelong matter. We can be fully assured of salvation today as we trust in Jesus, but growth in wisdom and maturity is a lifelong journey.

Model and encourage honesty with your children – if you can't give a full answer to one of their questions, say so, and take some time to research and find the answer. Some questions that might arise will be answered later in this course.

One of the enemies of faith is pretence. Don't expect your children to give 'pat' answers all the time or to pretend faith in public. The reality of their faith is more important than portraying some kind of religious perfection. When one of our children was going through a time of doubting God's existence, we met with their Christian teacher to get permission for them to respectfully ask to pass for a time when asked to pray in class.

7. Application and prayer

Pray briefly at the beginning of your family devotion time, thanking God for his presence and asking for his guidance.

At the end of your time together, ask your children what has stood out to them. Encourage them to make that matter the subject of prayer, asking God to help them apply it to their lives. If they don't yet know Jesus, encourage them to talk to God about that, or pray for them yourselves.

A prayer is also provided at the end of each week's reading which you may choose to use as an alternative. Talk with your children about your own answers to prayer, including when the answer was 'no' and about what God has done in your life. Don't wait until you are perfect – we are all a work in progress!

Here is a prayer you may wish to say (from the Anglican Diocese of Dunedin to be used before a hui or class):

> *E te Atua Kaha Rawa*
> *Hōmai ki a mātou te māramatanga me te mōhiotanga,*
> *Manaakitia mai mātou i ngā wā katoa.*
> *Korōria ki tō ingoa tapu.*
> *Āmine*
>
> *O God Almighty*
> *Give us understanding and knowledge*
> *Take care of us at all times*
> *May your holy name be glorified.*
> *Amen*

There is a well-known saying that 'a family that plays together stays together'. This can be expanded to, 'a family that plays, prays and serves together grows together'.

Now, let's get started!

Week 1

What things are wonderful to you?

A hobby I have taken up recently is woodturning – making bowls, rolling pins and similar items on a machine called a lathe. It is fascinating to watch a skilled craftsman putting a sharp tool to a piece of wood, seeing the turnings peel off, and producing wonderfully artistic and useful items like bowls, spinning tops and so on. The real wonder, however, is cutting into the piece of timber for the first time as it spins on the lathe and seeing the colours and patterns of grain revealed in the wood, especially after it is finished and polished.

It often strikes me that I am still just the second set of eyes to see that beauty. God, in his greatness, was already aware of each cell that made up the wood, and he created the beauty we see.

A scientist looking through a microscope at tiny animals or a high-country tramper coming across a flower on a remote mountainside also have the same privilege of seeing God's wonder through creation. Creation is full of wonderful things, whether it is in looking up at the night sky or at fireflies, examining rocks, diving under the ocean, or studying patterns of chemistry or genetics. These wonders tell us that there is Someone behind the beauty – Someone higher than ourselves – and that life is about more than just what we can touch and see.

The Bible tells us in Ecclesiastes 3:11 that God 'has planted eternity in the human heart'. Eternity is something that is hard for us to imagine. How do we understand something that goes on forever and ever? What more is there to life than what we can see and experience in our lifetime? Why has God put a sense of eternity into our hearts?

In Acts 17:26-28a, Paul spoke to the very educated Greeks in Athens, saying: 'From one man he created all the nations throughout the whole earth. He decided beforehand when they should rise and fall, and he determined their boundaries. His purpose was for the nations to seek after God and perhaps feel their way toward him and find him – though he is not far from any one of us. For in him we live and move and exist.' Paul was saying that God wanted the Athenians to know him and have a relationship with him.

When a sense of wonder strikes us from something we see or experience, it is important we don't just forget it and move on. We should think about how it was made, why it was made and who made it. God wants us to ask questions and seek answers. Proverbs 25:2 says: 'It is God's privilege to conceal things and the king's privilege to discover them.' This verse applies to our Christian journey – it is good to ask questions, and God has made us curious so we might find a relationship with him as our Creator.

Although we can't fully understand God with our minds, God wants us to use our minds to get to know him. The Bible also tells us that God is a Spirit and that we have also been made with a spirit inside us to communicate with him.

Shortly after I committed my life to Jesus in my late teens, a crystal-clear thought suddenly came into my mind. A question came first: 'What if I have got all of this wrong and there is no God, and what if all I have come to believe about Jesus Christ isn't true after all?' As quickly as the question came, the answer followed: 'Even if I have got all of this wrong, it is still the best way to live.' I have found God more real year by year, and following the teachings of the Bible means life makes more sense and goes better, even if there are difficulties at times. I believe God not only wants us to have a relationship with him but has made us to live in a particular way, according to the Bible, even if it is hard or unpopular at times. Any other way of living is less than the best that he wants for us.

Further reading: John 1:1-5; Revelation 4:9-11

What things are wonderful to you? (Week 1)

✏️ To answer

1. Fill in the missing letters in these sentences:

God has planted eternity in our hearts to help us f _ _ d h _ m.

'...the glory of kings is to d _ _ _ _ _ _ r things.'

2. Look in this Word Find to find five things God has made. The words could read in any direction: up, down, backwards or sideways.

T	D	N	I	W
R	K	C	O	R
E	W	A	H	Z
E	Y	T	O	X
Q	D	R	I	B

💬 To discuss

1. What do you think this phrase means: 'God has planted eternity in the human heart'?

2. How does knowing that God has made beautiful things help us understand his plans for our lives?

3. How or where can you find answers to your questions about God?

▶️ To do

A circle (like a wedding ring) goes on forever, like eternity. Tie a knot in a piece of string to make a loop like a ring. Learn how to tie useful knots like those at www.animatedknots.com. You might want to start with a reef knot. Talk together about what you think eternity with God might be like.

 **Prayer**

Our Heavenly Father and our God, thank you that you have made us to wonder and to ask questions. Thank you that we are always in your thoughts. Please help us to always find our way to you through your son, Jesus. We ask this in his name, Amen.

Week 2

What is God like? Part 1

If you think back to when you first heard about God, what did you think he was like? Did he look like us? Where did he live? As a child, I thought God was like an old man with a white beard and tall hat, sitting on a cloud way above the sky. That was probably my eight-year-old mind trying to make sense of being told that God lived in heaven somewhere and that he was more powerful than us.

The Bible tells us that no one has ever seen God. In Isaiah 64:4, we read: 'For since the world began, no ear has heard and no eye has seen a God like you, who works for those who wait for him!'

So, what is God like? The Bible says that God has revealed himself to us in Jesus. In 2 Corinthians 4:6, we read: 'For God, who said, "Let there be light in the darkness," has made this light shine in our hearts so we could know the glory of God that is seen in the face of Jesus Christ.'

God knew we would have difficulty understanding what he was like, so he sent Jesus. Jesus lived among us in human form and his favourite description of himself was the 'Son of Man', meaning that he was fully human. He could have chosen to talk about himself as the Messiah (or 'Rescuer') or Son of God because he was both of those things, too, but Jesus spoke about himself as 'Son of Man' so we could understand God the Father through him.

Here are some characteristics of God:

1. He has always existed and always will exist

We live in a world where time is very important – we have birthdays, seasons, Christmas, and Easter. Have you ever said to your parents while on a trip somewhere, 'Are we there yet?' Or have you ever had an experience you wished would never end? Perhaps a bottomless plate of ice cream or a holiday in a wonderful place.

The Bible tells us that there are special times in our lives that God plans. I can still clearly remember September 18th, 1973, at 6:35 pm, when Jesus first became real in my life. The Bible tells us these special times have a beginning and an end, like a person's life.

When the Bible talks about God, however, it says he has no beginning or end. Psalm 90:2 says: 'Before the mountains were born, before you gave birth to the earth and the world, from beginning to end, you are God.' Jesus said the same thing about himself in John 8:58: 'Jesus answered, "I tell you the truth, before Abraham was even born, I am!"' He meant that he was equal to God and had always existed.

2. He is the Lord of all the earth and heavens

We don't live in a society where we have lords in castles ruling over us. In medieval times, each country had a king, with lords under the king. Each lord also had peasants or ordinary people who they ruled over, and the peasants were expected to serve their lord and be obedient to his wishes. In the Bible, God is also referred to as Lord. In 1 Timothy 6:15, God is described as: 'the blessed and only almighty God, the King of all kings and Lord of all lords.'

At present, we see many people not obeying God, but Philippians 2:10-11 promises that one day, 'at the name of Jesus every knee should bow, in heaven and on earth and under the earth, and every tongue declare that Jesus Christ is Lord, to the glory of God the Father.'

3. He is all-powerful or 'omnipotent'

The Bible tells us in many places that God is more powerful than any other human or being. Just as we learn about other people by the kinds of things they do, in Genesis 1, we see that God is powerful through the creation of the heavens and earth out of nothing. We also see his power through the miracles he does. He moved the seas to give the Israelites a way of escaping the Egyptian army and sent lightning down to consume the sacrifice Elijah had put on the altar on Mount Carmel. Job said in Job 42:2: 'I know that you can do anything, and no one can stop you.'

In John 2, we read that during his ministry, Jesus helped prevent a family from being embarrassed by turning water into wine at a wedding feast. In Mark 4:35-41, we read that he calmed the storm on Lake Galilee. In Mark 10:27, Jesus said to the disciples: 'Everything is possible with God.'

We especially see God's power in the resurrection of the Lord Jesus after his death on the Cross. In Ephesians 1:19-20, Paul prays for the Ephesians: 'I also pray that you will understand the incredible greatness of God's power for us who believe him. This is the same mighty power that raised Christ from the dead and seated him in the place of honour at God's right hand in the heavenly realms.'

4. He is the Creator and the sustainer of life

As we have already discussed, God made everything we can see around us. Isaiah 40:28b says, 'The Lord is the everlasting God, the Creator of all the earth.' God also keeps everything he has made working properly. Psalm 145:15-16 says: 'The eyes of all look to you in hope; you give them their food as they need it. When you open your hand, you satisfy the hunger and thirst of every living thing.' Talking about Jesus in Colossians 1:17, we read: 'He holds all creation together.'

Further reading: Isaiah 9:6; Psalm 145:3; Ephesians 1:19-21; 1 Timothy 6:15; Matthew 6:26

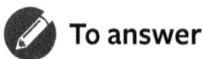
Growing in Jesus

✏️ To answer

Draw lines to match up the following lists:

God can do anything	God is eternal
God feeds the birds	Jesus is Lord of all
God has everything under control	God is omnipotent
God has always been alive	God cares for what he has made

💬 To discuss

1. Philippians 2:10-11 says that one day, everyone will acknowledge that Jesus is Lord. Why do you think God isn't making that day happen now?

2. God keeps all creation going. What does this teach us about his care for us?

3. Knowing that God is all-powerful, what is he asking you to trust him for in your life?

▶️ To do

Wine, as Jesus made, is fermented using yeast. Ginger beer also uses yeast, though different types that don't make alcohol. Find a recipe for ginger beer and make some together as a family. Talk together about God's miracles.

🙏 Prayer

Our Heavenly Father and our God, we praise you for your greatness and power in what we see you have made. Thank you that you show us your care through Jesus. Please give us your strength and help in what we do this week that others may see you in our lives. We pray this through Jesus, our Lord and friend. Amen.

Week 3

What is God like? Part 2

When he lived on earth, Jesus looked very ordinary. We read about him in Isaiah 53:2b that: 'There was nothing beautiful or majestic about his appearance, nothing to attract us to him.' Although we can't see God and don't know what Jesus looked like, we can learn about God and his character from what the Bible tells us about Jesus' life.

1. He is present everywhere at once or 'omnipresent'

Have you ever played hide and seek and thrown an object to make a noise to try and trick someone into thinking you are in a different place? We can only ever really be in one place at a time; however, God is Spirit and can be everywhere at once. Jeremiah 23:24 tells us: '"Can anyone hide from me in a secret place? Am I not everywhere in all the heavens and earth?" says the Lord.' There is nowhere we can go where God isn't there already, and he is with everyone in the world at the same time.

During his ministry on earth, Jesus could only be in contact with a few people at once. In John 16:7-8, he said to the disciples: 'But in fact, it is best for you that I go away, because if I don't, the Advocate won't come. If I do go away, then I will send him to you. And when he comes, he will convict the world of its sin, and of God's righteousness, and of the coming judgement.'

Jesus was talking about the Holy Spirit (or Advocate), who was sent to earth after Jesus went back to heaven after his resurrection. In that way Jesus, by his Spirit, can be with all believers around the world at the same time.

2. He is all-wise, knows all things or is 'omniscient'

If you are fortunate, you might have a grandparent you can ask questions of because no matter how smart parents are, they don't know quite everything! With God, we can all have someone whom we can ask questions of and who does know everything. Not only that, but he will always listen. In Psalm 147:5, King David wrote: 'How great is our Lord! His understanding is beyond comprehension!'

John 1:18 tells us that Jesus makes God known to us, and he invites us to find all the wisdom we need for life in a relationship with him. Many times, Jesus showed wisdom in answering the Pharisees' tricky questions and helping people come to know God.

In John 4:1-26, he understood that the woman who came to get water from the well really needed her inner thirst satisfied, and in Luke 18:18-22 Jesus saw that wealth was preventing a rich young man from following God even though he was living a righteous life.

3. He is holy – He is perfect and wonderful

Read these verses:

Revelation 4:8 'Each of these living beings had six wings, and their wings were covered all over with eyes, inside and out. Day after day and night after night they keep on saying, "Holy, holy, holy is the Lord God, the Almighty - the one who always was, who is, and who is still to come."'

'Holy' isn't a word we use very much, but if we look it up in the dictionary, we find it can mean 'dedicated to God, or perfect in goodness'.

In the Bible, the word 'holy' has a slightly different meaning from just perfectly good. It is used to refer especially to God. It means he is more wonderful than anyone or anything else we have ever seen, and this showed in Jesus' life when people were changed just by being with him.

Jesus showed God's holiness by living a perfect life. Every part of Jesus' character is holy – his love when he healed people, his forgiveness when he spoke to people who had sinned, and even his anger when he rebuked the hypocrisy of the religious rulers.

4. He is good to us

You might have received a school report with a tick in a box beside 'good', meaning that you had reached a certain standard in reading or maths or sport. But what does the word 'good' mean when the Bible uses it about God?

Other gods that were worshipped either in Old Testament days or in the Greek and Roman times were often changeable, meaning that they were believed to do good sometimes or harm at other times. In contrast, when God is described as 'good', it means he is always morally and ethically perfect.

Psalm 25:8 says: 'Good and upright is the Lord; therefore, he instructs sinners in the way.' It also means there is nothing evil or even unpleasant about God. His thoughts and actions toward us are always for our best.

Jesus revealed the goodness of God's nature to us when he lived on earth. In Mark 7:37, after healing a man born deaf and partly mute, the people said of Jesus: 'Everything he does is wonderful.' At his trial before Pontius Pilate, no one could find anything Jesus had ever done wrong to accuse him. Acts 10:38b tells us that: 'Jesus went around doing good and healing all who were oppressed by the devil, for God was with him.'

Further reading: Lamentations 3:22-26; Romans 8:28; Psalm 139:7-12; James 1:5-6

Growing in Jesus

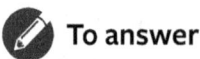 **To answer**

Choose answers from the list below to match up with each of these Bible stories:

Jonah praying in the whale.
Moses taking his sandals off at the burning bush.
Blind Bartimaeus healed by Jesus.
Solomon finding the true mother of a baby (1 Kings 3:16-28).

God is holy. God is everywhere. God is wise. God is good.

 To discuss

1. How does knowing that God is everywhere help us think about where we can pray and what we can pray about?

2. How does knowing that God's thoughts and actions toward us are always for our good help us to trust him?

3. God is omniscient or all-wise. Is there an area of your life or a decision you have to make that you could ask for God's wisdom?

 To do

At night, in a room in your house, try to make it as dark as possible by stopping all the light coming in. Talk together about how God can turn darkness into light.

 Prayer

Our Heavenly Father and our God, thank You for being so wise and wonderful. Please help us this week to show your goodness to others by following Jesus' example and with his help. We ask this through him. Amen.

Week 4

What is God like? Part 3

We finished last week by looking at God's goodness and thinking about how God's character never changes. Even if we sin, which we will do from time to time, God doesn't change. 2 Timothy 2:13 tells us: 'If we are unfaithful, he remains faithful, for he cannot deny who he is.' That means we can come back to God at any time, ask for his forgiveness, and receive it. Hebrews 13:8 also says: 'Jesus Christ is the same yesterday, today, and forever.'

Mark 2:2-11 tells the story of a paralysed man whose friends lowered him through a hole they made in the roof of a house because there was no other way of getting near to Jesus. Jesus first forgave the man his sins, so he was right with God and then healed him so he could stand up and carry his bed home.

1. He is just in all he does.

Justice and righteousness are two words that are closely linked in the Bible. Justice refers to how we obey God's ways and how we should treat others. Righteousness is a similar word to justice, but it mostly refers to how Jesus' death has made us right with God.

Deuteronomy 32:4 says of God: 'He is the Rock; his deeds are perfect. Everything he does is just and fair. He is a faithful God who does no wrong; how just and upright he is!' Justice, as it is taught in the Bible, is the basis of many of our laws. In the end, however, only God is perfectly just, as we can easily see!

There is so much injustice in the world, but God also promises in the

Bible that sometime in the future, all unjust treatment will be put right. This means there will be a day when God judges the whole earth. We read in Psalm 96:13b: 'He will judge the world with justice, and the nations with his truth.' Only God is completely just, and only he is qualified to be the judge of all people.

When each of us stands before God, our judgement will be based first on how we have responded to the Lord Jesus. Jesus promised in Matthew 10:32: 'Everyone who acknowledges me publicly here on earth, I will also acknowledge before my Father in heaven.'

There is an important difference between the Christian faith and other religions when it comes to justice. In other religions, for mercy to be shown, sin and, therefore, justice must be overlooked, as justice isn't done without a penalty being paid for sin. In contrast, God doesn't ignore justice when he shows mercy, and this is because he bore all our sins on the Cross when Jesus died on our behalf.

Justice and mercy are brought together for us in the Lord Jesus.

2. He is loving and kind

God's nature is that of love, and all his actions toward us come out of his love. God's love is so deeply a part of his nature that the Apostle John says in 1 John 4:8b: 'God is love.' God's love is the best thing we can experience, above any human love from parents or others.

God also responds to us when we love him by trusting and obeying him. In Psalm 91:14, we read: 'The Lord says, "I will rescue those who love me. I will protect those who trust in my name."'

Although God, our Father, is in heaven, he is with us by his Spirit and wants a two-way relationship with us based on love. In Psalm 63:3, we read: 'Your unfailing love is better than life itself; how I praise you!' Our response to God comes from the overflow of his love in our hearts.

God is also kind, meaning he understands what we need and how we feel, and he acts toward us to help us. Kindness is a practical action that helps someone, not just a feeling. God is also kind even when we don't deserve it, as we read in Romans 2:4b: 'Can't you see that his kindness is intended to turn you from your sin?' The greatest practical act of kindness ever shown was when God gave his Son for us.

3. He is the source of all truth

Truth in the Bible means more than getting an answer right in a test at school. It means more than all knowledge or practical wisdom. Truth means what is real in life as God originally made it. Truth always comes from the person of God and Scripture and won't be contradicted by anything science finds out about our planet and the universe. Psalm 119:160 tells us: 'The very essence of your words is truth; all your just regulations will stand forever.'

Most importantly, truth tells us about the purpose of life – why we are here and how to know God. Jesus came to show us God and he is the truth. In John 14:6, Jesus said: 'I am the way, the truth, and the life. No one can come to the Father except through me.' Because God has revealed truth in Jesus, we can be assured that following him will lead to the real life God intends for us.

4. He is merciful toward us

Mercy is kindness shown toward someone when it isn't deserved. Because Jesus died to take the penalty for our sins, God offers mercy toward everyone who will choose to receive his forgiveness. Psalm 103:10 says: 'He does not punish us for all our sins; he does not deal harshly with us, as we deserve.' We experience God's mercy when we are forgiven again and again. The Bible also encourages us to show mercy to others who have done things against us.

Further reading: John 3:17-18; Matthew 7:1-2; Psalm 103:10-12; Psalm 119:160; John 8:32

Growing in Jesus

✎ To answer

Match up these two lists:

1. Treating others according to God's ways   A. kindness
2. Something that is right and real   B. truth
3. Helping another person   C. mercy
4. 1 John 4:8   D. loving
5. Something that we don't deserve   E. just

💬 To discuss

1. Why is it that God can show mercy toward us?

2. Jesus taught things that were true even if many people disagreed with him. How does knowing he is with us help us do the right thing even when it is unpopular?

3. It is sometimes harder to be kind to the people we are closest to. How can we act in a way that shows we are made in God's image?

▶ To do

This week, think about an action you can take that shows God's character in one of the ways we have learned about. Talk together about how God's mercy and kindness help us to follow him.

🙏 Prayer

Our Heavenly Father and our God, thank you that you love us so much! Please help us when we are unfairly treated. Help us also to show the same love and forgiveness to others as you show us through Jesus, who died to save us. Amen.

Week 5

What did God do in creation?

The first Christian belief described in the Bible is the creation story in Genesis, where we read that God made the heavens and the earth out of nothing. My career has involved studying and teaching science, and when I was seeking to know God, believing in creation was a barrier to me because it seemed to be the opposite of what I had been taught.

What got past that barrier for me was coming to know Jesus Christ as a living person and believing that if God could bring his Son, who was dead, back to life, then creating life and order out of nothing wasn't a problem for him. Just how and when God created the earth didn't matter so much as my belief that he could do it.

It's reassuring that discoveries in science don't contradict the biblical record, but it's still important that we have faith in what the Bible says on its own. In Hebrews 11:3, we read: 'By faith we understand that the entire universe was formed at God's command, that what we now see did not come from anything that can be seen.' With faith in God as Creator, the Bible story makes sense, and our faith helps us to grow in faith in God and to become more like Jesus.

We can see the wonder of what God has made in creation both in large and small things. On Christmas Day 2021, the James Webb telescope was launched, and it arrived at its destination about 1.5 million kilometres from Earth in January 2022. It started sending pictures back to Earth six months later. With its larger mirror and infrared design, the telescope can detect objects up to 100 times better than the older Hubble telescope, and it can show us objects near the edge of the known universe.

Growing in Jesus

We read in Psalm 89:11-13: 'The heavens are yours, and the earth is yours; everything in the world is yours – you created it all. You created north and south. Mount Tabor and Mount Hermon praise your name. Powerful is your arm! Strong is your hand! Your right hand is lifted high in glorious strength.'

In Genesis 1:2a, we read: 'The earth was formless and empty, and darkness covered the deep waters.' Although God existed before creation, all the different types of atoms that make up the universe didn't exist. So, God created everything in the universe out of nothing.

In a similar way, in Jesus' healing miracles, he made healthy skin for the lepers and a new eye to make the blind man see. What God did in creation shows us his character and how he would have us live. For example, he brought light, and he brought order. When we live our lives by obeying God's Word and making good decisions, we are living in the light, and we experience order and peace in our hearts, even if we are going through problems.

Here are some other things that God did in creation:

He made time and seasons.
He made plants, animals and other living things that could reproduce.
He made living things with an ability to survive in changing environments.
He made different kinds of ecosystems to work together.
He made beauty to be enjoyed.

It is wonderful that God has made beauty in so many places to be enjoyed by him and by us and for that beauty to bring praise from our hearts. Revelation 4:11 says: 'You are worthy, O Lord our God, to receive glory and honour and power. For you created all things, and they exist because you created what you pleased.'

It is God's nature to be creative, and although he finished making the earth and its living things after six days, he continues to do creative things. We read in Isaiah 42:9 (ESV): 'Behold, the former things have come to pass, and new things I now declare; before they spring forth I tell you of them.' God continues to do new things every day, and he has made us to be creative like him and look after what he has made.

In addition to what we can see with our eyes or through a space telescope, God has placed laws in creation that scientists can discover for our benefit, and we can give glory to God for.

The creation story tells us more about God, and we read in Scripture how the three persons of the Godhead worked together to make creation. Firstly, the Father, in Genesis 1:1: 'In the beginning God created the heavens and the earth.'; secondly, the Son, Jesus, in John 1:1-3: 'In the beginning the Word already existed. The Word was with God, and the Word was God. He existed in the beginning with God. God created everything through him, and nothing was created except through him.' And finally, the Holy Spirit, in Genesis 1:2b: 'And the Spirit of God was hovering over the surface of the waters.'

God shows us his goodness by looking after or renewing his creation so it doesn't break down. We read in Psalm 104:30: 'When you give them your breath, life is created, and you renew the face of the earth.'

1 Peter 4:19 says: 'So if you are suffering in a manner that pleases God, keep on doing what is right, and trust your lives to the God who created you, for he will never fail you.' As God sustains his creation, this helps us to trust his promise to care for us.

Lastly, although humans have done a lot of damage to creation, God also promises that in the future, he will make all of creation new again when the Lord Jesus returns to earth for the second time. Isaiah 65:17 says: 'Look! I am creating new heavens and a new earth, and no one will even think about the old ones anymore.'

Further reading: Psalm 148; Isaiah 40:26; Isaiah 43:18-19; Isaiah 44:24; Genesis 1:28

Growing in Jesus

 To answer

Read Genesis 1 and match these sentence beginnings and ends by drawing lines:

On day one, God made...   ...day three.
God made the heavens on day...   ...the animals and people were made.
The plants were made on...   ...day two.
The sun and moon were made...   ...light.
Last of all...   ...on the same day.

 To discuss

1. How can the ways we look after creation show that we are followers of Jesus?

2. The Bible promises that one day God will make a new heaven and new earth. What do you think they will be like?

3. What are five things you can praise God for?

 To do

Use a magnifying glass to look at the patterns on items like an insect wing (it's best to find one already dead), a leaf, and a very thin slice from a cork. God also made very big things like the stars. Go outside on a clear night and find the Southern Cross. Learn how to use it to find true south. The Southern Cross is seen on the New Zealand, Australian and Samoan flags. Talk together about how creation teaches you about God.

Prayer

Our Heavenly Father and our God, we praise you for the beautiful world we live in. Please help us to look after it well until the Lord Jesus returns and you make it all new again. For your name we pray, Amen.

Week 6

How did God create humans?

While studying entomology (insects) at university, I was fortunate enough to find a species of ground weta that was new to science. It wasn't new to me, as we had been seeing them burrowing for years in the garden, but it caused some excitement for one of my lecturers, who got to describe it in a scientific paper.

In reading Genesis 1, we see that God made weta and most other animals on day six, with the aquatic animals and birds made the day before on day five. Sometime during day six, after he had made weta and about two million other species, God changed direction and spent special time on the very last species to be made – us.

We read in Genesis 1:26-27: 'Then God said, "Let us make human beings in our image, to be like us. They will reign over the fish in the sea, the birds in the sky, the livestock, all the wild animals on the earth, and the small animals that scurry along the ground." So God created human beings in his own image. In the image of God he created them;
male and female he created them.'

There is a second description of God creating humans in Genesis 2:7. We read: 'Then the Lord God formed the man from the dust of the ground. He breathed the breath of life into the man's nostrils, and the man became a living person.' As God breathed into us, he gave us a spirit, a way of being aware of God and of being in relationship with him that no other living thing has.

God has also shaped each one of us personally with his hands and has a special plan for our lives, as we read in Psalm 139:15-16: 'You watched me as I was being formed in utter seclusion, as I was woven together in the dark of the womb. You saw me before I was born. Every day of my life was recorded in your book. Every moment was laid out before a single day had passed.'

The book of Genesis in the Bible has been described as the 'book of beginnings', not just the beginnings of life but also the beginnings of most major Christian beliefs and teaching. What we believe and live as Christians must be true to the patterns God gives us in the Bible for us to experience the best that God plans for us. Anything different from those patterns or his plan takes glory away from God, and we miss out on the blessing he wants us to experience.

So, what does it mean to be made in God's image? The Bible tells us that no one has ever seen God, so it must mean something other than looking like him. Being made in God's image means God wants his character to show up in our lives. Only humans can make moral decisions, to decide if something is right or wrong. We have a conscience, an inner voice that tells us if we are about to lie or steal something or if we have spoken or acted unkindly to another person.

Ephesians 4:24 says: 'Put on your new nature, created to be like God – truly righteous and holy.' This is the new life we receive when we come to know Jesus. While I was writing this, my wife Linda was making a meal for someone in need rather than spending time on her hobbies. God has made us like this to be able to put the needs of others before our own.

Being made in God's image also means we are made to trust him in every area of our lives, both for the forgiveness of our sins through Jesus and by living according to his teaching in the Bible. We will read later that Adam and Eve missed out on the wonderful life that God planned for them when they made a wrong decision to disobey one of God's commands. This wrong kind of independence shows up in all of us when we don't listen to God.

While God gave Adam the job of giving names to all the animals, he named Adam himself, giving him a name meaning 'mankind' or human.

We also read in Genesis 1:27 that God said: 'So God created human beings in his own image. In the image of God he created them; male and female he created them.' When God had finished making Adam, He took a 'side' or an aspect from Adam to make Eve, as we read in Genesis 2:21-24.

This tells us that God makes men and women different from one another from when they are born. As a result of creation, men and women are somewhat different, not just in their bodies, but often in other ways.

In the world today, some people say we should question the gender we are born with. God promises, however, that if we trust in how he has made us, we will know the security and reassurance of his plan for our lives; even though sometimes it may be difficult and confusing for a while, and take time to work through. There are wonderful passages that reassure us about following God's Word rather than trusting human wisdom.

Proverbs 3:5-8 says, for example: 'Trust in the Lord with all your heart; do not depend on your own understanding. Seek his will in all you do, and he will show you which path to take. Don't be impressed with your own wisdom. Instead, fear the Lord and turn away from evil. Then you will have healing for your body and strength for your bones.'

This promise is not just that a broken arm will heal up, but it means a deep inner peace and strength that comes from living our lives in obedience to Scripture as we grow in the Lord Jesus.

Further reading: Psalm 139:13-14; Psalm 102:18; Ephesians 2:10

Growing in Jesus

✏️ To answer

Put true or false beside these five sentences:

1. God made humans from the dust of the ground.

2. We can trust how God has made us.

3. Humans and animals can both pray.

4. God has made people before he made weta.

5. Our conscience is given to us to help us obey God's commands.

💬 To discuss

1. How can we get to know God as our friend?

2. How does knowing that God has a special plan for each of us help us trust the way he has made us if we have doubts?

3. How can the ways we relate to others in our daily lives show that we are made in God's image?

▶️ To do

Use clay, play dough or plasticine to craft the head and face of someone else from your family. Talk together about how God has made each of us special and unique.

🙏 Prayer

Our Heavenly Father and our God, thank you for making each of us individually and that you have a special plan for each one of us. Please help us to always trust in your plan for our lives, knowing that you will never let us down. Through Jesus we pray. Amen.

Week 7

What is God's will for us?

Imagine you heard that someone was going to join your class at school or youth group at church. Also imagine you were told they were the best at everything – the fastest runner, the smartest, as well as the best musician. They were so much better at all those things that no one else had ever beaten them. You might feel it would be hard to have them around because you would always feel inferior or not as good as them.

But what if when they turned up, they asked to be your best friend? You found that they were such a good friend and helped you out with so many things that it didn't matter that they won everything. Because they were such a good friend, you were happy that they did well.

In 1648, the churches of Britain published the *Westminster Catechism* (a book of Christian beliefs and teachings). It has about 100 questions and answers. The very first question is: 'What is the chief end (or purpose) of man?'. The answer is: 'Man's chief end is to glorify God, and to enjoy him forever.' To glorify God means that we give him praise because he is wonderful, and we understand we owe all we are or ever will have to him.

Remember the woodturning I mentioned earlier, which I do as a hobby? Say I produce a fruit bowl for someone as a gift. It has a beautiful grain, is a nice shape, and is smooth and polished. I might get praise for having made it, but I think back to Bob, who taught me woodturning and what a well-shaped bowl looks like. Then there are the people who made the special steel so my chisels will hold a sharp edge and the engineer who built the lathe I work on.

Most of all, I remember God, who made the wood with the beautiful patterns and gave the tool and machine makers the intelligence to make what they did. When I think about it, my part in making the bowl is really quite small.

When we glorify God, we turn the attention off ourselves and onto him. As we do that, his attention comes to us in return, and we can feel how wonderful and what a blessing it is to have him as our best friend.

Isaiah 43:7 tells us that our purpose in life is to bring glory to God, and in Colossians 3:17, we read that '... whatever you do or say, do it as a representative of the Lord Jesus, giving thanks through him to God the Father.' God wants us to have a thankful attitude and to trust him for his help in all the little and big things we do each day. How do we do that?

In 1 Thessalonians 5:17, we are told to: 'Never stop praying.' Now this doesn't mean we should spend our whole day on our knees with our eyes closed, but rather that we should trust him for help and guidance and depend on him throughout the day. One way is to shoot 'arrow prayers' up to God for his help. That glorifies God and works out for our best too, even if it takes a while for God's answer to our problem to arrive. Another very important way we glorify God is by thinking about the needs of others before our own.

What about the second half of the answer to that question in the Westminster Catechism, where we are invited to 'fully enjoy him forever'? How do we enjoy God when we can't see him or touch him, and sometimes, when we don't feel that he is with us? Jesus says in John 15:13-15: 'There is no greater love than to lay down one's life for one's friends. You are my friends if you do what I command. I no longer call you slaves, because a master doesn't confide in his slaves. Now you are my friends, since I have told you everything the Father told me.'

The first and most important way we enjoy God is by receiving his love for us by dying on the Cross so that we might come to know him. That brings us peace with God as we know we have been forgiven. Secondly, we know God's joy as we learn about and follow the example of the Lord Jesus. In John 15:11, Jesus says: 'I have told you these things so that you will be filled with my joy. Yes, your joy will overflow!' How wonderful it is to know love, peace and joy in our hearts and minds that lasts!

We also use the word 'hope' quite often when we are talking about something that we want to happen in the future but that we aren't quite sure of. We might hope to get into a particular sports team or to go somewhere for a holiday in summer.

For a Christian, our hope to be with God in heaven in the next life will definitely happen because God has promised it to us in Jesus. Some things that happen in this life are not enjoyable, and there will be times when we struggle to know the enjoyment and closeness of God's love, peace, and joy. God's presence now and in the future, however, is assured.

Finally, Romans 5:3 tells us: 'We can rejoice, too, when we run into problems and trials, for we know that they help us develop endurance. And endurance develops strength of character, and character strengthens our confident hope of salvation. And this hope will not lead to disappointment. For we know how dearly God loves us, because he has given us the Holy Spirit to fill our hearts with his love.'

I have learned that many times God hasn't taken away my problems, because he wanted me to learn how to trust him in the problems. Also, he has been shaping me to become more like Jesus.

Further reading: 1 Peter 4:11; 1 Corinthians 10:31; Romans 5:1-5; John 16:33; John 15:11

Growing in Jesus

✏️ To answer

Use peace, love, hope or joy to finish or start these sentences.

1. Jesus wants our hearts to be filled with his _____

2. When God forgives us, we have _____ with him.

3. Jesus died for us because of his _____

4. _____ means that we will live forever with God.

💬 To discuss

1. Why does God want us to glorify him?

2. What does God promise us when we glorify him?

3. The Bible tells us to rejoice in God always. Is there a difficulty you are having where you can rejoice that God is still with you?

▶️ To do

Make a bow and arrow. To make the bow, use a plastic coat hanger with the hook cut off and use duct tape to reinforce the plastic so it won't break. Loop together a few rubber bands to use as the bowstring. Use drinking straws for the arrows. Talk together about something you could shoot arrow prayers to God about.

🙏 Prayer

Our Heavenly Father and our God, thank you that you want us to know your love and to have you as our best friend. Help us always to glorify you so that others can see your greatness. In the name of your son Jesus, we ask this. Amen.

Week 8

Where do we find God's will?

When I was a new Christian learning about finding God's will, I remember praying about a 50-cent decision but not about buying a brand-new $1000 motorcycle on hire purchase! Although God promises to guide us in the big and small things of life, his will is much more about how our character is being changed to become like the Lord Jesus, as we read about him in the Bible. His will is that through love, we give him first place in our lives and love others as ourselves.

When Jesus was asked by the Pharisees what the greatest commandment was, he replied in Matthew 22:37-39: 'You must love the Lord your God with all your heart, all your soul, and all your mind. This is the first and greatest commandment. A second is equally important: "Love your neighbour as yourself."' If we seek to obey these two commands each day, we won't go far wrong in following Jesus.

A few years later, I was finishing Teachers' College and ready to apply for my first teaching job. My father was ill, and I read this verse in 1 Timothy 5:8: 'But those who won't care for their relatives, especially those in their own household, have denied the true faith. Such people are worse than unbelievers.' It was clear to me that I should look for a position in a school near home where I could also help my parents with Dad's ill health, and God provided that.

Where do we find the instructions for making good decisions and becoming more like Jesus? As we've already seen, God has given us the Bible as an inspired written record of how he wants people to relate to him. The Bible isn't an ordinary book, as it says that the human writers were inspired by God's Spirit. As we read its words, they are the words of God to us as he speaks to our hearts and gives understanding to our minds.

When the Apostle Paul was writing to Timothy in 2 Timothy 3:16-17, he said: 'All Scripture is inspired by God and is useful to teach us what is true and to make us realise what is wrong in our lives. It corrects us when we are wrong and teaches us to do what is right. God uses it to prepare and equip his people to do every good work.'

Sometimes the Bible won't make sense to us, though. I remember trying to understand the New Testament a couple of years before I came to faith in Jesus. I just couldn't get into it or understand what I was reading. We must know the God who inspired it for it to have meaning in our lives.

We must also be willing to obey the message of Scripture. In Psalm 32:8-9, we read: 'The Lord says, "I will guide you along the best pathway for your life. I will advise you and watch over you. Do not be like a senseless horse or mule that needs a bit and bridle to keep it under control."' A horse tends to run off and be harder to control, while a mule is famous for being stubborn and difficult to get moving.

If we either run ahead of God or aren't ready with his help to obey what we read in Scripture, his words won't reach our hearts and we won't grow spiritually. My motorcycle purchase was probably the 'running ahead of God' type of decision!

Living by God's will as shown to us in the Bible produces a life that is pleasing to God and experiences his blessing. The Bible has been described as a manual for life. We might read a manual when we buy a new bread maker to find instructions for setting it up for different recipes, and for help when things go wrong. The Bible contains the instructions from our Maker for us to live life the best way.

Joshua 1:8 contains a wonderful promise for us: 'Study this Book of Instruction continually. Meditate on it day and night so you will be sure to obey everything written in it. Only then will you prosper and succeed in all you do.' What does this mean for us?

Where do we find God's will? (Week 8)

Sometimes, listening to preachers on TV, it seems that it should mean having more than enough money and being free from difficult circumstances in life. From Scripture, though, the more important areas are having victory over sin, putting God first in our choices by trusting and obeying him, and learning to be unselfish toward others.

The most important time to learn these lessons starts when we are young. Ecclesiastes 12:1a says, 'Don't let the excitement of youth cause you to forget your Creator. Honour him in your youth'. Putting God first in our lives sets a good foundation for the future. Before I was married, I spent a year at bible college to grow in God's ways and spent time in mission outreach rather than dating, trusting that God would bring my future wife and I together in his time, which he did.

In some areas, temptations are also stronger when we are younger, but the Bible has some wonderful passages for young people. Psalm 119:9, 11: 'How can a young person stay pure? By obeying your word. I have hidden your word in my heart, that I might not sin against you.' And later in verse 105: 'Your word is a lamp to guide my feet and a light for my path.'

Joshua, who we looked at earlier, led the people of Israel into the Promised Land. He learned about God's plan for his life when he was younger by spending time praying in the tabernacle tent. He gained experience in leadership by helping Moses and showed that he trusted God by obeying his commands in smaller things first.

Further reading: Deuteronomy 6:1-3; Joshua 1:7-8; Psalm 119:9-16; Proverbs 3:5-6

Growing in Jesus

✏️ To answer

Match these sentence beginnings and ends by drawing lines:

In our hearts...	...we spend time with him.
To get to know God...	...to help others.
We make good decisions...	...we learn to trust God.
The Bible gives us light...	...to overcome sin.
God helps us...	...to show us God's way.

💬 To discuss

1. In what way is the Bible different from every other book?

2. If we learn to obey God through the teachings of the Bible, how might this help us avoid harm in our lives?

3. Are you getting to know God through reading the Bible? If not, how might you do this regularly?

▶️ To do

Some people say there are contradictions in the Bible. Have a look at www.josh.org/. Talk together about what you find.

🙏 Prayer

Our Heavenly Father and our God, thank you for giving us the Bible, so that we can read your words and learn about you. Help us to take your words right into our hearts and show in our actions so the Lord Jesus might shine out through us. In his name we pray. Amen.

Week 9

Who is Jesus?

In the time of the early church, a teacher called Arius began to teach that Jesus wasn't equal to God but instead was like a created 'super angel'. This error has persisted today in groups like Jehovah's Witnesses and Mormons, who have similar beliefs to Arius.

Why is it so important to understand and believe that Jesus is the Son of God and equal to the Father? Essentially, if Jesus was only an angel, he couldn't have paid the price for the sins of the world. It would also have been morally wrong for God to sacrifice someone else rather than pay the price for sin himself.

Jesus reveals God the Father to us. A few weeks ago, we looked at how hard it is for us as humans to understand what God is like. By learning about the life of Jesus, we can do that – we can know and experience God the Father personally, through Jesus, with the help of the Holy Spirit.

Hebrews 1:1-5 tells us about Jesus and how he is superior to angels. How many ways can you count in these verses?

'Long ago God spoke many times and in many ways to our ancestors through the prophets. And now in these final days, he has spoken to us through his Son. God promised everything to the Son as an inheritance, and through the Son he created the universe. The Son radiates God's own glory and expresses the very character of God, and he sustains everything by the mighty power of his command. When he had cleansed us from our sins, he sat down in the place of honour at the right hand of the majestic God in heaven. This shows that the Son is far greater than the angels, just as the name God gave him is greater than their names.

The Son is greater than the angels for God never said to any angel what he said to Jesus: "You are my Son. Today I have become your Father." God also said, "I will be his Father, and he will be my Son."'

The Lord Jesus is greater than all other living things on earth. This includes all the men and women who have spoken, written and acted on behalf of God in the past. Jesus is greater than the chief angel Michael and the angel Gabriel, who announced Jesus' birth to Mary.

He is also much greater than the evil spirit, Satan, and the fallen angels who follow him in rebellion against God and who try to trick us away from God. So, how is Jesus greater? First, he existed before creation and will always live. Also, the final message of how to be saved that God has spoken is given through Jesus.

The Oxford Learner's Dictionary tells us that 'divine' means: 'coming from or connected with God.' Here are some of the things the Lord Jesus did during his ministry on earth that prove he is the divine Son of God:

- He forgave sins.
- He accepted worship from people who recognised that he was the Son of God.
- He performed miracles in his own name.
- He won against death.
- He lived a morally and ethically perfect life.
- He overcame and freed people from evil powers.
- He fulfilled many prophecies from the Old Testament.
- He changed the lives of his disciples.

As a matter of interest, there is far better evidence for the existence of Jesus Christ than for Julius Caesar (remember the Asterix books?) and other well-known people who lived about the same time as Jesus.

Jesus taught with an authority and wisdom that was recognised by his hearers, meaning that he was more than just an ordinary person. While most major world religions teach that doing good and gaining wisdom leads to salvation, only Jesus claimed that he himself was the way of salvation.

Jesus referred to God as his Father over 150 times. For example, in John 10:30, Jesus said: 'The Father and I are one.'

In John 14:9, Jesus said to Philip: 'Have I been with you all this time, Philip, and yet you still don't know who I am? Anyone who has seen me has seen the Father! So why are you asking me to show him to you?' By his life and his words, the Lord Jesus showed us that as the Son of God, he was divine or of the same substance or essence as the Father.

Let's look at some practical examples. In Luke 8:43-48, when Jesus healed the woman who was bleeding, he showed us that God was caring and compassionate. In Matthew 8:28-34, when he cast out evil spirits from the men at Gadarene, he showed that God had authority over all powers. In Luke 15:11-32, when he told the parable of the prodigal son, he showed that God was forgiving and able to restore people's lives. In Matthew 21:12-17, when he cleared the temple of the traders and moneychangers, he showed that God was just and the judge of all. When he taught and when he answered his critics, he showed the wisdom of God.

From the beginning, with Adam and Eve, all people have shown at some point that they want to do or say things that are against God's holy and loving nature. Because God is a God of justice as well as love, a penalty for our sin had to be paid, and it was by taking that punishment himself as the Son of God that a way was made for us to be restored to friendship with God. God loved us so much that he gave his Son to take our punishment for sin on the Cross.

Further reading: Isaiah 9:6; Matthew 1:23; John 14:16-17; Psalm 2:7; Matthew 3:17

Growing in Jesus

✏️ To answer

Choose words from the list below to finish these sentences:

1. Jesus is the son of _____ .

2. The Lord Jesus said that if we have seen him, we have also seen the _____ .

3. Hebrews 1 tells us that the Lord Jesus is more powerful than _____ .

4. Jesus shows us what God is _____ .

5. Jesus lived a perfect life without _____ .

List of words: sin, angels, Father, like, God.

💬 To discuss

1. What was it about the way Jesus lived and taught that made people believe he was the Son of God?

2. How does it make you feel knowing that Jesus is more powerful than anyone or anything else?

3. Is there something in the bullet points on page 58 that you would want Jesus to do for you?

▶️ To do

Google a list of human genetic features. Most features are dominant or recessive. Pick a few features and see how they have been passed down in your family to show up in you. (Because some features are recessive, they may be hidden for a generation or two). Talk together about the character features our Heavenly Father wants to see in our lives.

Who is Jesus? (Week 9)

 **Prayer**

Our Heavenly Father and our God, thank you that Jesus came to show us what you are like. We thank you that he shows us your love, power and care for us. We praise you Lord Jesus that there is no one else like you! Amen.

Week 10

What are angels and what do they do?

Many people have shared stories of angels who have played a part in their lives, perhaps by protecting them or giving them a message from God. Billy Graham, the great American evangelist, told many stories of angels in his book *Angels: God's Secret Agents*. Angels can appear in the form of ordinary people who appear at an important time to give us God's guidance in a tricky situation. They can also appear in their heavenly glory to frighten enemies who might be attacking us.

Angels are created by God as we are, though they are more powerful than us. Because angels are created beings and not divine in any way, we are not to worship or pray to them. When we pray to God, he may send angels to help us.

A missionary friend in Thailand was walking on a track near some bush one day when a large snake attacked her. A man who had passed her earlier suddenly ran back and stamped on its head and chased it away. She believes this man was probably an angel. The passages about angels in the Bible and people's stories like this convince me that angels are real and still operating in this world. Let's look at what the Bible says about angels and some stories that show how God uses them to help us.

In Genesis 28, we read the conversion story of Jacob at Bethel. He was running away to Haran after cheating his brother Esau out of his birthright and hearing that Esau was planning to kill him. As he slept, he dreamed of seeing angels going up and down on a ladder between earth and heaven. For the first time in his life, he became aware that God was real, and he promised to follow him.

Hebrews 1:14 tells us that angels are 'only servants – spirits sent to care for people who will inherit salvation.' Like Jacob, when we need to know God or pray for our friends to come to know him, angels may be part of how God answers prayer.

We also read in Psalm 91:11 that God sends his angels to protect us. 'For he will order his angels to protect you wherever you go.' In Acts 5:19, when the apostles were imprisoned for preaching the gospel, an angel was sent to open the prison doors and lead them out. Later in Acts 12, we read the story of how, after killing the Apostle James, King Herod had Peter arrested again, no doubt intending to kill him also. Again, as the church prayed for Peter, an angel rescued him. It wasn't until he was outside the prison on the street that Peter realised that the angel had been real and that he was free again.

We are very familiar with the angels in the Christmas story. First, an angel appeared to Mary, telling her that she would become pregnant and give birth to the Son of God and Saviour of the world. Joseph also received a visit from an angel telling him of what God was doing. At the time of Jesus' birth, an angel appeared to the shepherds in the fields and then a whole choir of angels sang praises to God.

In the Old Testament, in Daniel 8, we read that the angel Gabriel was told to bring a message to him from God to explain the visions that he had seen. Later in Daniel 10, another message was brought to Daniel by an angel, but we are told that first this angel had to be helped by a more powerful angel called Michael. Daniel had been fasting and praying for three weeks before Michael came to help get the message to him from God.

We can learn from this that there are times when we need to keep praying and trusting God to answer our prayers for some time. Our prayers and faith are important because there can be an unseen battle that must be won before the answer comes from God. Angels may be involved in getting the answer for the person we are praying for.

God can use angels to guide us. Joseph, the husband of Mary, was warned in Matthew 2:13: 'After the wise men were gone, an angel of the Lord appeared to Joseph in a dream. "Get up! Flee to Egypt with the child and his mother," the angel said. "Stay there until I tell you to return, because Herod is going to search for the child to kill him."'

After the people of Israel left Egypt and were journeying to the promised land, they were given a promise by God in Exodus 23:20: 'See, I am sending an angel before you to protect you on your journey and lead you safely to the place I have prepared for you.' In Acts 8:26, the evangelist Philip was given guidance to meet the Ethiopian eunuch by an angel.

God uses angels to care for us when we have a special need; for example, after the Lord Jesus had fasted for 40 days in the wilderness and been tempted by Satan, we read in Matthew 4:11 that: 'Then the devil went away, and angels came and took care of Jesus.' There is a similar story in 1 Kings 19:4-8. Elijah had just been told Queen Jezebel had promised to kill him, and he was feeling exhausted and depressed when God sent angels to miraculously revive his spirits. We read that an angel cooked Elijah a special meal that enabled him to travel for forty days.

Lastly, the Lord Jesus taught in Matthew 18:1-2,10 about how each child has a guardian angel: 'About that time the disciples came to Jesus and asked, "Who is greatest in the Kingdom of Heaven?" Jesus called a little child to him and put the child among them. "Beware that you don't look down on any of these little ones. For I tell you that in heaven their angels are always in the presence of my Heavenly Father."'

Further reading: 1 Kings 19:4-8; Daniel 10:1-14

What are angels and what do they do? (Week 10)

 **To answer**

Put these sentences from the Christmas story in the right order:

The shepherds ran to Bethlehem.
An angel told Mary she would become pregnant.
A choir of angels sang to the shepherds.
An angel told Joseph to flee to Egypt.
An angel told Joseph to marry Mary.

 **To discuss**

1. What main job do angels have?

2. In what situation do you think God might send an angel to help you in answer to prayer?

3. Sometimes angels carried a message from God that he wanted people to obey. Is there something that you know God wants you to obey this week?

 **To do**

Follow these instructions to make some paper angel chains:
www.auntannie.com/Christmas/PaperAngels/

You might want to use coloured paper and keep them for Christmas decorations. Talk together about how we can always trust God to help us when we are in need.

Prayer

Our Heavenly Father and our God, we thank you that the angels you have made are one of your ways of helping us. Please strengthen our faith to know you are with us always, even when we don't feel your presence. We ask this in the strong name of Jesus. Amen.

Week 11

How does God watch over our lives?

One of the most wonderful things about the Christian faith is that God seeks us before we even think of looking for him. In Genesis, we read that when Adam and Eve sinned and hid from God, he went looking for them. In Luke 19:10, Jesus said: 'For the Son of Man came to seek and save those who are lost.'

In 1890, Francis Thompson published a poem called *The Hound of Heaven*. He tells the story of God following after a person who is running away from him. They try to hide from God in nature, in sin, and in human love. In the end they come to realise that in all the difficulties caused by sin, God has also been speaking to them in kindness. They finally realise that only by giving their whole heart to God would they ever find the comfort and meaning they were seeking.

A friend of ours studied this poem as a young person while she was trying to run away from God. One night, shortly before she became a Christian, she awoke tangled in the bed sheets – she had been running from God in a dream.

In Psalm 139, we read that there is no place where we can hide from God – verse 12 says that even darkness is light to him. In verse 16, we read: 'You saw me before I was born. Every day of my life was recorded in your book. Every moment was laid out before a single day had passed.' We are always in God's thoughts and all his thoughts toward us are for good.

God's often unseen actions in our lives have been called his 'providence'. God's providence has been defined as: 'his caring provision for his people as he guides them in their journey of faith through life, accomplishing his purpose in them'. It is wonderful that God has been seeking us before we even knew about him or had begun to seek him.

Shortly after the last supper that Jesus shared with his friends after he rose from the dead, he went to heaven and sat down at God's right hand. Even there, he still helps us. Romans 8:34 tells us that Jesus is praying for us: 'Who then will condemn us? No one – for Christ Jesus died for us and was raised to life for us, and he is sitting in the place of honour at God's right hand, pleading for us.'

Earlier in verse 26, we read: 'And the Holy Spirit helps us in our weakness. For example, we don't know what God wants us to pray for. But the Holy Spirit prays for us with groanings that cannot be expressed in words.' Not only is Jesus praying for us in heaven, but God's Spirit helps us to pray.

Although we can't see God's Spirit, his presence can be known and felt in our hearts and minds. He also works in other ways to show us God's care. In John 14:16, we read: 'And I will ask the Father, and he will give you another Advocate, who will never leave you.' The word 'advocate' means someone who comes beside us and helps and supports us. Later in verse 26, Jesus promises: 'But when the Father sends the Advocate as my representative – that is, the Holy Spirit – he will teach you everything and will remind you of everything I have told you.'

Let's look at some other ways God watches over our lives and works for our good.

If we sin and let God down, 2 Timothy 2:13 tells us that: 'If we are unfaithful, he remains faithful, for he cannot deny who he is.' Hebrews 13:5b says of God: 'I will never fail you. I will never abandon you.' Sometimes when I feel I have let God down most badly, I am most aware of his love and help as I have turned to him again. The Apostle John writes in 1 John 1:8-9: 'If we claim we have no sin, we are only fooling ourselves and not living in the truth. But if we confess our sins to him, he is faithful and just to forgive us our sins and to cleanse us from all wickedness.'

We can easily see that the world is affected by sin in many ways. Friends and neighbours can argue, people in business can be greedy, and politicians can think more about having power than those they should be serving. Sometimes, all of this means that bad things happen to good people. This hurts, and we can ask ourselves or God the question: 'Why?'

While we may not always understand the reason, we have God's promise to turn it into good. Romans 8:28 says: 'And we know that God causes everything to work together for the good of those who love God and are called according to his purpose for them.' If we trust and obey God, who is wiser and more powerful than us, He will bring good out of every situation.

In the Bible, God sometimes describes himself as an eagle. In Exodus 19:4, we read: 'You have seen what I did to the Egyptians. You know how I carried you on eagles' wings and brought you to myself.' Eagles have eyesight that is about eight times better than ours. They also have the advantage of being able to fly high so they can get a 'bird's eye' view! That tells us that God can see what is ahead of us in life, so we can trust him in difficult times.

Isaiah 40:30-31 says: 'Even youths will become weak and tired, and young men will fall in exhaustion. But those who trust in the Lord will find new strength. They will soar high on wings like eagles. They will run and not grow weary. They will walk and not faint.'

Further reading: John 15:16; Philippians 1:3-6; 2 Thessalonians 2:16-17; Romans 8: 31-39

How does God watch over our lives? (Week 11)

✏️ To answer

1. Can you remember two ways the Holy Spirit helps us?

2. What is Jesus doing in heaven now? Is he:

a) resting   b) praying   c) chasing after us   d) hiding from us

3. How does it make you feel knowing that God can see what is ahead of you? How could you pray about this?

💬 To discuss

1. What do you understand God's providence to mean?

2. How does it make you feel to know that God is watching over your life?

3. Is there something difficult in your life at present you could ask God to carry for you?

▶️ To do

Carry a raw egg around with you for a day. Think of ways you can look after it so it doesn't get broken. Talk together about what you have learned about God's care for you.

🙏 Prayer

Our Heavenly Father and our God, knowing that you will never fail us or abandon us is so wonderful! Thank you for your Holy Spirit who stays close to us and that we can always turn to you for help. Through our Lord Jesus we pray. Amen.

Week 12

What does it mean that God has a plan for my life?

We have just had our grandchildren visiting and we love spending time with them! Whenever we see them, they are a little bigger and smarter as they journey to adulthood, and we wonder what they will do when they are grown up. We wonder what gifts God has placed in their lives, and every day we pray that they will come to love and follow Jesus.

One of the most important human needs is to know that our lives have significance. We are made with a desire to know that our lives have meaning and that we are valued, loved and appreciated. What does the Bible have to say about this?

Psalm 139:16 says: 'You saw me before I was born. Every day of my life was recorded in your book. Every moment was laid out before a single day had passed.' These words tell us that while God is all-powerful and has made the universe, he also has a plan for each one of us. His love and care watches over every detail of every moment of every day. The first step to having significance in our lives is having a relationship with the God who made us.

The way we do this is to choose to trust in Jesus as our Lord and Saviour. In Matthew 4:18-22 we read about Jesus calling his first four disciples to leave their old lives and follow him. Once they did that, he spent three years teaching the disciples to do the work of bringing others to him. These disciples were quite uneducated and came from poor backgrounds, giving us encouragement that God specialises in using anyone who will receive his love and depend on him.

Romans 8:29 says that God not only calls us to follow Jesus but also chose us 'to become like his Son.' We are specially and lovingly called by God to overcome sin and to gradually become like Jesus in our attitudes, words and actions. To do this, we need to spend time regularly reading the Bible, praying and obeying God's commands. Psalm 119:1-2 says: 'Joyful are people of integrity, who follow the instructions of the Lord. Joyful are those who obey his laws and search for him with all their hearts.'

Although God has designed us to work together with others, he also has a plan for each of us as individuals. In Jeremiah 1 we read about God calling a young man to speak a message to the people of Israel. Even though Jeremiah was quite young, God had given him unique gifts and had a specific plan for his life.

Matthew 10:29-31 says that we are so valuable to God that he has numbered every hair on our heads! If God knows this much detail about us, he also knows what gifts and talents he has placed in our lives to serve him and others. Sometimes we may not have recognised those gifts yet, but as we grow in faith while following Jesus, God will give us opportunities to discover and use them. It can take some time to adjust and become confident in doing something new, but if God has designed us to do something we will find we enjoy it.

God's plans for our lives often turn out differently from the way we expect. As we follow Jesus, the path will often have unexpected twists and turns, delays and surprises. In Acts 16 Paul and Silas were stopped from going to two different places before they found the place God was calling them to go. Although God puts long-term desires in our hearts (e.g. to go into business, to work in missions or to be an artist), he reveals it to us step by step. That is because he wants us to learn to know him and depend on him and to become like Jesus along the way.

A Bible verse that we often hear when God's plans are discussed is Jeremiah 29:11 which says: '"For I know the plans I have for you," says the Lord. "They are plans for good and not for disaster, to give you a future and a hope."' These words were written to God's people who were in a very difficult place as exiles in a foreign country. We can be reassured by this verse that even if life is difficult and we don't feel God's presence, he is still there and thinking of us. God can even turn our difficulties into something good, as he works out his plan for our lives.

Lastly, Isaiah 30:21 is a wonderful promise from God to guide us in his plan for our lives. We read: 'Your own ears will hear him. Right behind you a voice will say, "This is the way you should go," whether to the right or to the left.' Over the years as I have tried to learn and obey God's plan in my life, I have learned to hear him more clearly and to love his voice. Some parts of that plan have happened very quickly, while others have taken many years. That doesn't matter to me because knowing his presence and knowing that I am pleasing him are the most important things.

It is exciting to discover and explore what gifts God has given us, and to find out what adventures he has in store for us.

Further reading: Hebrews 12:1-2; Jeremiah 18:1-5; Jeremiah 1:5

What does it mean that God has a plan for my life? (Week 12)

 **To answer**

Unjumble the underlined backwards words in these sentences:

God sevol me. He has a nalp for my efil. He gave me stfig to serve him and pleh others.

 **To discuss**

1. How is every individual person important to God?

2. What has God done that shows that you are important to him?

3. Think of a gift you might have. How could it glorify God, help others and bless you?

 **To do**

Play the board game 'Snakes and Ladders'. Talk together about how this might be similar to and different from God's plan for a person's life.

Prayer

Our Heavenly Father and our God, thank you for caring enough for us that you made us and gave Jesus to die for us. We praise you that you have made us for a purpose. Please help us glorify you and the Lord Jesus by following your plan. Amen.

Week 13

What happened when Adam and Eve were tempted to do wrong?

Some years ago, our family lived in northern Thailand for a year and loved the wonderful variety of fresh tropical fruit we could buy at the markets. Mangos were a special favourite. When we returned to New Zealand, we were disappointed that the only tropical fruit we could get were a few high-priced mangoes, frozen durian, or tinned lychees. They were a poor substitute for what we had left behind in Thailand.

In Genesis 3, we read how Adam and Eve were sent out of the fruitful garden of Eden after they sinned. They lost not just a perfect garden but the presence and friendship of God. Genesis 3:23 describes the sad result of their sin: 'The Lord God banished them from the Garden of Eden, and he sent Adam out to cultivate the ground from which he had been made.'

How did this happen? Although Adam and Eve were without sin at first in the Garden of Eden, sin was still present in the form of Satan. Satan sought to take over God's place as ruler of the world he had created. His first step was to tempt Eve to eat the fruit of the tree of the knowledge of good and evil, the only tree that God had commanded Adam and Eve not to eat from.

In the next part of the story in Genesis 3:1-6, Satan, in the form of a serpent, spoke to Eve and twisted God's words by saying: 'Did God really say you must not eat the fruit from any of the trees in the garden?' He then tempted Eve to pride and to disobey God when he said: 'God knows that your eyes will be opened as soon as you eat it, and you will be like God, knowing both good and evil.' Eve gave in to that temptation, and shortly after, Adam did also.

Satan's strategy in tempting Eve had three parts to it. First, he questioned what God said. He said: 'Did God actually say...?'

The Bible is unlike any other book as it is inspired by God, and he speaks to us through his Spirit. The Bible points us to salvation and helps us grow to become more like Jesus. Satan still uses ideas which seem clever but are outside of the Bible in order to tempt people. We need to be careful to keep a belief in every part of Scripture and trust God for understanding if we have questions. 2 Timothy 3:16 tells us: 'All Scripture is inspired by God and is useful to teach us what is true and to make us realise what is wrong in our lives. It corrects us when we are wrong and teaches us to do what is right.'

Secondly, Satan questioned God's goodness. He twisted what God said by implying God had said: 'You must not eat the fruit from any of the trees in the garden.' God is not a spoilsport who wants to take away from our lives and make us miserable. Certainly, there are times when he will tell us to stop certain things that are not good, but he will always give us something better if we obey him.

Thirdly, Satan tempted them by saying that there would be no consequences to their disobedience. He tempted them into taking the fruit of the tree that God had forbidden but didn't say what would happen if they disobeyed God by eating it. At that time, Adam and Eve had never experienced evil, but every action has a consequence. Galatians 6:7 tells us: 'Don't be misled – you cannot mock the justice of God. You will always harvest what you plant.' Whatever good or bad we do will have an outcome at some point in the future. Unfortunately, Adam and Eve were deceived, and their sin and disobedience produced terrible consequences in their lives.

So, from where Adam and Eve knew God's presence and had everything they needed, they now understood the evil that came from their disobedience. We call this 'The Fall' as Adam and Eve fell from the wonderful relationship with God that they had previously enjoyed. The first thing they did was to hide from God. They felt shame and fear they hadn't known before.

At the same time, they also experienced parts of God's character they had not known. They experienced rebuke and judgement and were sent out of the Garden of Eden and from God's presence. Even before they were sent out, however, God began the process of bringing humankind back to himself by making them garments of animal skin. This action showed the sacrifice God would make for all people by giving Jesus to die in their place.

The sin of Adam and Eve also shows up in our sinfulness and separation from the life of God. We read in Romans 5:12: 'When Adam sinned, sin entered the world. Adam's sin brought death, so death spread to everyone, for everyone sinned.' Through Adam and Eve's sin, this spiritual death has spread down through the generations to all of us. Each of us shows through our actions that we are sinners, too, along with Adam and Eve. However, we can't finish the story there!

The good news is the life of God that comes into us when we commit our lives to the Lord Jesus is much stronger than our tendency to sin. Romans 5:15 says: 'But there is a great difference between Adam's sin and God's gracious gift. For the sin of this one man, Adam, brought death to many. But even greater is God's wonderful grace and his gift of forgiveness to many through this other man, Jesus Christ.'

Further reading: Psalm 51:5; Romans 3:23; Romans 6:23

What happened when Adam and Eve were tempted to do wrong? (Week 13)

 **To answer**

Think of words or actions that are 'better than' those on the left (the first one is done for you):

Criticising	Encouraging
Boasting	
Leaving someone out	
Giving up	
Answering back	

 To discuss

1. What are the truths the Bible tells us that are different from what Satan said to Adam and Eve?

2. How does it help us to remember that Jesus has already defeated Satan?

3. Satan tells lies about God and about life. Are there any lies we have heard that we need to be careful not to get tricked by?

 To do

Make a mango lassi together. You can blend a tin of sliced mangoes and add yoghurt and sugar and cardamon to taste. For a dairy-free option, substitute coconut yoghurt or coconut cream. Talk together about how God invites us to be close to him again.

 Prayer

Our Heavenly Father and our God, thank you that though we have been cut off from you by sin, you offer a new life in the Lord Jesus. Please help us to follow your word that shows us the best way to live. Through Jesus we pray. Amen.

Week 14

What is sin?

Imagine you are at a friend's house, and you are invited to take an apple from a bowl. Which one will you take? Will it be the reddest one, or the largest, or just the one that is nearest to you? One lesson stuck in my mind from the first Easter camp I attended as a new Christian. Pastor Rex Tito was speaking, and although I don't remember much of what he said, the lesson about the bowl of apples stuck in my mind. He said to take the worst-looking apple as a way of putting the needs of others before our own. Often, the battle against sin is also one against our own selfishness.

As we have seen, temptations to sin often run deeper than just which apple to choose. The temptation to Adam and Eve was really about the deeper issue of who would be in charge in their lives. Would they obey God's command not to eat of the tree of the knowledge of good and evil, or would they choose to live by their own rules?

When we come to faith in the Lord Jesus, God will start the process of gradually changing us to be more like him. At first, more obvious matters are dealt with – perhaps our language, our obedience to our parents or the way we treat our siblings. Later, God works on our attitudes to others and motives for what we do. Although we often see sin as something done wrong against another person, every time we treat someone else badly, we are also sinning against God.

King David wrote Psalm 51 in repentance after he had slept with another man's wife and then tried to cover it up by arranging the man's murder. David wrote in Psalm 51:4: 'Against you, and you alone, have I sinned; I have done what is evil in your sight. You will be proved right in what you say, and your judgement against me is just.' The main point we need to understand about any sin is that it is first committed against God and his character. David sinned by committing murder, which broke one of the Ten Commandments God has given to us.

People sometimes justify a decision to do something outside the teaching of Scripture, for example, a wrong relationship, by saying it does 'no harm' to another person. However, any wrong choice, including those where we do economic harm to others, is first an offence against God. Ultimately, it is God whom we will each have to stand before to explain how we lived.

So, what does sin against God involve? Psalm 19:7 says: 'The instructions of the Lord are perfect.' God's Word, the Bible, contains commands and teaching about every area of life – no aspect is left untouched. But perfection is about more than obeying God's commands. 2 Samuel 22:31a tells us: 'God's way is perfect.' God himself is perfect.

Not only is he without moral fault but he is whole and complete in himself or, simply put, he is holy. His character includes everything that deserves praise and is unimaginably wonderful. God wants us to obey him from our hearts because we love him above anyone and everything else.

Isaiah had a vision of God in Isaiah 6:1-3: 'It was in the year King Uzziah died that I saw the Lord. He was sitting on a lofty throne, and the train of his robe filled the Temple. Attending him were mighty seraphim, each having six wings. With two wings they covered their faces, with two they covered their feet, and with two they flew. They were calling out to each other, "Holy, holy, holy is the Lord of Heaven's Armies! The whole earth is filled with his glory!"' As a response to seeing this, Isaiah eagerly gave his whole life to God to serve him.

Moses also had a life-changing meeting with God at the burning bush in the desert, as recorded in Exodus 3. His friendship and intimacy with God reached such a level that when he came down from the mountain after receiving the Ten Commandments, his face shone with God's glory, and he had to wear a veil over his face to avoid frightening the people.

Songwriters through the centuries have written of God's beauty, with titles like 'O for a thousand tongues to sing', 'O worship the King, all glorious above', 'Immortal, invisible, God only wise', You are Beautiful Beyond Description', and so on. It might seem hard to grasp that people can write like this about a God we can't see or touch and when we are living ordinary lives, but God loves to reveal who he is to those who seek him.

So why do we humans continue to sin against God when he is so wonderful? Many people reject his authority over their lives as Creator; they contradict his truthfulness, doubt his goodness, judge others when he is the only Judge, hate instead of love, argue with his wisdom and turn their backs on his grace offered to us in the Lord Jesus.

Every command God has set out in Scripture for us to live by flows out of his love, his goodness, and his perfection. His commands are for our good and his glory at the same time. In his book, *The Weight of Glory*, C.S. Lewis said that each of us has the potential to become either 'immortal horrors or everlasting splendours.' We can choose to live in sinful disobedience to God, living as our own masters, or we can give our whole lives to him and experience his wonderful plans for our lives.

Further reading: Psalm 106:43; Psalm 101:5

What is sin? (Week 14)

✏️ To answer

Look up these Bible verses together and:

- decide what attitude is described
- decide whether the attitude is good or bad

Bible verse	Attitude	Good or bad?
Deuteronomy 15:9		
2 Chronicles 32:25		
1 Samuel 18:16-18		
1 Samuel 18:7-9		
1 Chronicles 28:9		
Philippians 4:2		
Ecclesiastes 7:9		

▶ To do

Stand up domino tiles or Jenga blocks to make the word 'Sin'. Push one tile of each letter over. Talk about how small actions that are sinful can have bigger consequences.

Talk together about how God has given us a conscience to protect us from the harm of sin.

🙏 Prayer

Our Heavenly Father and our God, we know that sin will always do us harm no matter how attractive it seems to be sometimes. Please help us to make right choices and to glorify you because you love us so much. Amen.

Week 15

How have humans and creation been damaged by sin?

Water bears, or as they are also called, moss piglets, are fascinating, tiny eight-legged animals about half a millimetre long, often found in mosses. They are found in many places, from deep oceans to the top of Mt Everest and even Antarctica and are regarded as the toughest animals known to science. They can survive temperatures from minus 273° to more than 150° Celsius as well as the vacuum and radiation conditions of outer space. God has also made them to be able to go without food and water for 30 years.

We live in a time when there is much concern about the future, including major issues such as climate change and extreme weather events. God is not caught by surprise by these things, and Jesus often spoke reassuringly about the future. For example, he said in John 16:33: 'I have told you all this so that you may have peace in me. Here on earth you will have many trials and sorrows. But take heart, because I have overcome the world.'

Jesus doesn't pretend that difficult times won't come, but he does promise to be with us in them and that we will come out on the winning side. Perhaps how God has made the water bears can also speak to us about his power and ability to look after us. And just as God cares for all his creation, Christians should be good conservationists as we imitate him and think of the needs of others. An example in the Bible is that the people of Israel were banned from cutting down food-producing trees when they needed timber.

Trees appear in many places in Scripture. The trees of life and the knowledge of good and evil are at the beginning of the Bible, in Genesis, and at the end of the Bible, in Revelation, the tree of life appears again, bearing twelve kinds of fruit for healing. Deuteronomy speaks about a curse being carried on a tree. This is a symbol of Jesus bearing our sins on the Cross.

As recorded in Exodus 15, in their journey from Egypt to the Promised Land, the Israelites found undrinkable water, and God performed a miracle for them through Moses when he threw wood into the waterhole, making it drinkable. Rongoā – or the medicinal use of plants like kawakawa, manuka, rangiora and koromiko by Māori is knowledge that God has revealed for our good.

In addition to healing, creation teaches us about God's grace and mercy. Living things are connected in many ways in a food web, and if one source of food disappears for an animal, they can switch to others, ensuring their survival. Jesus reminded us that God's care for us is much more even than his care for the animals.

After the Fall in the Garden of Eden, God said that Adam and Eve would have to always work hard to get food from the earth. This was a prediction of the damage humans would do to the environment in their efforts to live without God. Romans 8:19-23, however, promises that one day, all of creation will be restored by God when Jesus returns. God promises to give us new bodies and to undo the damage that has been done through sin.

Until Jesus returns, we can glorify God and show love to others by being good stewards of what he has made. As Christians, we focus first on remembering God, then on loving our neighbour, rather than just focusing on creation itself. In Matthew 22:39, the Lord Jesus said: 'Love your neighbour as yourself.'

I once taught students who were working on a science fair project to solve a problem in their home village in Samoa. Rising sea water was spoiling their coastal gardens, and they were trying to find a way to love others by experimenting with different ways of growing food. When things become depleted and Māori place a temporary ban or rāhui on harvesting a resource for a period of time, this action loves others by letting the resource recover to feed people again in the future.

There are many passages in the Bible about what will happen in the end times before the Lord Jesus returns to set up his kingdom on earth. The Bible teaches about a time when all that is on the earth will be brought before God and judged. In 2 Peter 3:10, we read: 'But the day of the Lord will come as unexpectedly as a thief. Then the heavens will pass away with a terrible noise, and the very elements themselves will disappear in fire, and the earth and everything on it will be found to deserve judgement.'

When this passage speaks of fire, it refers to how fire reveals what things are made of. If something made of metal and wood is burned, the wood will be burned away but the metal will remain. The Bible tells us that if we belong to Christ, we will be protected in his care, and the things we have done in his name, even unseen kind deeds, will show up.

Finally, in Revelation 22:1-3, we see the tree of life appear again. We read these wonderful words: 'Then the angel showed me a river with the water of life, clear as crystal, flowing from the throne of God and of the Lamb. It flowed down the centre of the main street. On each side of the river grew a tree of life, bearing twelve crops of fruit, with a fresh crop each month. The leaves were used for medicine to heal the nations. No longer will there be a curse upon anything. For the throne of God and of the Lamb will be there, and his servants will worship him.'

For those who follow Jesus, all the effects of sin, including sickness, harm and the damage to creation will be undone, and there will be no barriers to being in God's presence. People will be fully healed and restored, and a new earth will be made.

Further reading: 2 Peter 3:1-13; Hebrews 12:26-27; Revelation 21:1-4; Romans 8:19-23

How have humans and creation been damaged by sin? (Week 15)

To answer

Find the names of the New Zealand animals hidden in this Word Find:

F	E	H	A	K	A	T
U	C	J	O	D	H	U
R	O	B	I	N	Q	A
S	N	A	F	Y	G	T
E	R	K	I	W	I	A
A	T	E	W	Z	L	R
L	P	A	X	U	S	A

To discuss

1. As Christians, how can we show that our care of creation reflects our love for God?

2. In what ways do you think the new heavens and earth God promises might be different from the ones we have at present?

3. Is there a beach or riverbank nearby you could help clean up by collecting plastic rubbish? Sort the plastic afterwards for recycling.

To do

Collect a small clump of moss, wet it with tap water, and wait 20 minutes. Squeeze the water into a flat glass dish and let the mud settle. Water bears are see-through, so put black paper under the dish to help you see them. Search the dish using a hand lens, a smartphone camera with a macro lens, or a microscope if you have one. Talk together about the wonderful world God has made that we can enjoy.

 Prayer

Our Heavenly Father and our God, your creation shows us so much about your wisdom and power. Please help us to look after it for your glory and that Jesus may be seen through our lives. Amen.

Week 16

What remedy did God provide for Adam and Eve's sin?

For two summers as a university student, I worked at a freezing works in the beef slaughterhouse. When I first started, all the blood and gore was a bit of a shock, and I remember for the first week or two I only took cucumber sandwiches for lunch. They were the least like meat that I could think of! I quickly adjusted, however, and learned some useful skills.

Cooking programmes on television nowadays often talk about respecting every part of an animal that has died for us. Death is a solemn thing and is a central theme of Scripture, leading to the Cross. As we begin reading the Bible, it doesn't take many pages before things start going wrong. Adam and Eve sin, and their relationship with God is broken. As we read further on in the Bible, however, we see there is a road map given to lead us back to God.

The sin Adam and Eve committed resulted in God's judgement because he is a God of justice, and he must act consistently with that part of his character. A wrong done requires a penalty to be paid, and this happened at the Cross. The first thing we read God doing after Adam and Eve were judged for their sins was making clothes for them out of animal skins, beginning to point to when the Lord Jesus was to die on the Cross for us. Let's look a bit more at what was done at the Cross.

Imagine you get caught writing on a desk at school. Your punishment is to clean the desktops for half an hour after school. Obediently, you arrive in the classroom, only to find that your teacher has allowed a friend to go in at lunchtime to substitute for you. They have given their time to pay the penalty in your place, and you are allowed to go straight home!

Theologians talk about a 'scarlet thread of redemption' running through the Bible, with the idea of a substitute taking the punishment for our sins. Later, when the people of Israel were given the law through Moses, they were commanded to make various sacrifices for their sins, also pointing to Jesus' future death for us. (The sacrificed animals also helped provide food for the tribe of Levites who served the people, as they didn't have land to grow food on.)

The idea behind the sacrifices was one of 'atonement' or 'at-one-ment', meaning that through their faith in God, the people would be made 'at one' with God again by the sacrifice of another life for their sins.

Redemption is another word the Bible uses for God to bring people back to himself. Atonement means our sins are forgiven, but redemption describes how God 'buys us back' by paying a price. Once we are redeemed, we belong to God, and a whole new life starts.

Job was a man who lived centuries before the time of Christ, somewhere near the land of Israel. Job went through incredible tragedies in his life, but through these, he learned more about the power and wisdom of God. While still in the middle of his difficulties, Job made this statement in Job 19:25: 'But as for me, I know that my Redeemer lives, and he will stand upon the earth at last.' Job was inspired by God to know that there would be a time when Jesus would come down from heaven to earth and would redeem us.

Another person in the scarlet thread of redemption was a woman called Rahab. She lived in the city of Jericho when the Israelites were travelling from Egypt and beginning to conquer the Promised Land. Although she had a shady background, she came to trust God and was offered a new life among the people of Israel if she hid two spies. The spies promised she would be kept safe if she hung a scarlet cord out of the window of her house.

Afterwards, she was so changed that she married and became one of the ancestors of the Lord Jesus. The scarlet cord led to her being saved when the city was conquered and is now a symbol for us of the sacrifice of Jesus.

We also have the story of Abraham in Genesis 22:9-14. God tested his faith by commanding him to sacrifice his only son, Isaac. It was never God's intention for Isaac to die, so this was a test of Abraham's faith.

We read: 'When they arrived at the place where God had told him to go, Abraham built an altar and arranged the wood on it. Then he tied his son, Isaac, and laid him on the altar on top of the wood. And Abraham picked up the knife to kill his son as a sacrifice. At that moment the angel of the Lord called to him from heaven, "Abraham! Abraham!" "Yes," Abraham replied. "Here I am!" "Don't lay a hand on the boy!" the angel said. "Do not hurt him in any way, for now I know that you truly fear God. You have not withheld from me even your son, your only son." Then Abraham looked up and saw a ram caught by its horns in a thicket. So he took the ram and sacrificed it as a burnt offering in place of his son. Abraham named the place Yahweh-Yireh (which means "the Lord will provide"). To this day, people still use that name as a proverb: "On the mountain of the Lord it will be provided."'

Just as God provided a substitute for Abraham, he has provided a substitute for us in the person of his Son, our Lord Jesus. God gives us new life from the moment we choose to believe Jesus died in our place and rose to life, and we commit our lives to follow him. 2 Corinthians 5:17 has this wonderful promise: 'This means that anyone who belongs to Christ has become a new person. The old life is gone; a new life has begun!'

Further reading: Psalm 103:10-14; Isaiah 1:18; Ephesians 1:7-8; Zechariah 3:1-5

Growing in Jesus

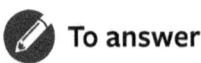 **To answer**

Choose the right word for the spaces to complete this cloze exercise:

We are made clean from sin by Jesus' _____ (blood/miracles/teaching). God _____ (hires/rents/buys) us back through Jesus dying for us. We are _____ (lost/free/tangled) to belong to God again.

 **To discuss**

1. What do you understand by the words 'redemption' and 'atonement'?

2. How do you feel about God giving his son for us?

3. 'We are not saved by good works but for good works.' Is there something you would like to do out of gratitude to God?

 **To do**

Make red dye together. You can use well-scrubbed beetroot or red rose petals or buy cochineal powder – made from ground-up scale insects. Once you have made a solution of the dye, use it to dye a piece of white cotton cloth. Once it's dry, you might want to drape it over a family cross. Talk together about how God washes the stain of sin out of our lives.

Prayer

Our Heavenly Father and our God, I am amazed that you would give your Son, Jesus, to die for me. Thank you that the blood of Jesus cleanses me from everything I have done wrong and give me a new life to belong to you. Amen.

Week 17

What does God's grace mean?

When Jesus was crucified on the Cross, there were two robbers also crucified beside him. They were possibly members of a bandit group who attacked and robbed travellers. At first, the two robbers joined in with the Jewish leaders in mocking Jesus, but after a while, one of them had a change of heart.

Luke 23:39-43 tells us the story: 'One of the criminals hanging beside him scoffed, "So you're the Messiah, are you? Prove it by saving yourself – and us, too, while you're at it!" But the other criminal protested, "Don't you fear God even when you have been sentenced to die? We deserve to die for our crimes, but this man hasn't done anything wrong." Then he said, "Jesus, remember me when you come into your Kingdom." And Jesus replied, "I assure you, today you will be with me in paradise."'

As he hung on a cross beside Jesus, the second robber came to realise two things. One, he was guilty before God for the wrongs he had done and two, Jesus was innocent of any wrongdoing. Perhaps that was because of Jesus' prayer forgiving those who were putting him to death, but somehow, this man recognised Jesus was truly God's Son sent to save him. Like others around that time, he would have heard stories of Jesus, who performed miracles of healing and doing good. Perhaps he had once sat on the edge of a crowd and heard Jesus teach?

What does this tell us about grace? The robber knew he had done wrong and that after he died, he would meet God and face judgement. He knew it was too late to do anything to save himself, but something drew him to ask Jesus for help and trust in him.

The word 'grace' means something given by a person in a higher position to someone in a lower position. As God is higher and we are lower, that means the generous act of grace is offered to us by God. We read in Ephesians 2:8: 'God saved you by his grace when you believed. And you can't take credit for this; it is a gift from God.' No matter how much good we do in our lives, we can't earn salvation by our own efforts. If we know we don't deserve to be Jesus' followers, then we will be invited to be with him as Jesus promised the thief on the cross beside him.

In Romans 5:20, we read: 'God's law was given so that all people could see how sinful they were. But as people sinned more and more, God's wonderful grace became more abundant.' This is wonderful news because even though our sin has terrible effects, God's grace has even greater power for good. Imagine the joy the robber would have felt as he found himself in paradise with Jesus!

Let's imagine what might have happened in his heart and mind as he talked with Jesus before he died.

- He had a repentant heart and was truly sorry for his sins.
- He was humble enough to ask Jesus for help.
- He trusted Jesus.
- Jesus promised he would be with him in paradise, so even though he was suffering on his own cross, he had joy in his heart.

What does grace mean for us who are still here following Jesus? Just as we are saved by grace, we also need grace to keep following him. In John 1:16, we read about the Lord Jesus: 'From his abundance we have all received one gracious blessing after another.' James 4:6 also says that God: 'gives grace generously.'

The parable of the prodigal son gives us an understanding of the welcome God gives us. The son came to his senses after sinning and decided to return home to his father. He knew he didn't deserve a place in the family as a son again but was hoping to be taken on as a servant. Instead, he was treated with amazing grace as his father ran to him, embraced and kissed him, and then put on a great party.

God's grace also gives us the gratitude and courage to be a witness to Jesus through our lives and words out of a desire to see others share what we have come to experience. In Acts 4:33-35, Peter and John had just had their first trip to prison for preaching the gospel. Grace not only gave them the strength to speak boldly about Jesus but also motivated the new believers to become a loving, serving community so no one among them was in need.

Finally, let's look at the example of Paul the Apostle. God called him to be an apostle, away from a life spent persecuting Christians, and he was always grateful to God. Later in his ministry, Paul experienced a problem he called a 'thorn in the flesh'. It may have been a health condition or opposition from a particular group of people.

Paul asked God several times to remove it, but finally, he became content to see it as a way to know God's grace. In 2 Corinthians 12:8-9, we read: 'Three different times I begged the Lord to take it away. Each time he said, "My grace is all you need. My power works best in weakness." So now I am glad to boast about my weaknesses, so that the power of Christ can work through me.' Paul experienced the grace of God both at the start of his Christian walk and later as he found God's strength helping his weakness.

Further reading: Luke 23:32-43; Ephesians 2:8; Romans 5:2; Titus 2:11; Matthew 20:1-16

Growing in Jesus

 To answer

Put these words in the right order for the acronym 'GRACE':

riches   expense   God's   at   Christ's

 To discuss

1. Jesus said that the thief on the cross would go straight to paradise after he died. What do you feel/think about that?

2. Is there something you have done in the past that you need to accept God's grace and forgiveness for?

3. Is there someone you know who would benefit from you showing God's grace to them?

 To do

Make a paper table mat. Decorate it to explain what grace means to you. Perhaps you could draw the father welcoming the prodigal son back home. Talk together about how God is full of joy when we return to him.

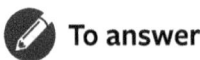 **Prayer**

Our Heavenly Father and our God, though we don't deserve it, we praise you for your grace. Help us to be thankful to you every day and to show grace to others. Through the Lord Jesus we pray. Amen.

Week 18

Why did the Lord Jesus need to become human?

Many people like reading comics or watching movies about superheroes who fight evil and injustice. Most of us have heard of characters like The Flash, Captain America, The Hulk, Superman, Batman, Wonder Woman, Spider-Man and so on. Superheroes, however, are not perfect. Some are proud or cruel, some are reckless, and many can't see their own faults.

Earlier, we looked at the Lord Jesus as the Son of God and how he reveals God the Father to us. Although he wanted people to believe in him as the Son of God, when Jesus spoke about himself, he used the phrase 'Son of Man'. He rarely spoke about himself as the Messiah or the Christ because the Israelites would be confused about what that meant. They were looking for a Messiah, like a superhero who would free them from Roman rule, rather than someone who would free them from their sins.

So, what did Jesus mean when he said: 'Son of Man'? Essentially, it simply means 'human', and we know that Jesus was born into the world as a baby, grew up, learned a trade, and lived among his family and friends as fully human. He ate, worked, made friends, got tired, and slept like everyone else. In his life, Jesus saw wrongdoing, suffering, illness, death, and hunger.

So, what does this mean for us? In calling himself the 'Son of Man' and being fully human, Jesus showed us that God was coming fully into our world to identify with us. Jesus lived just as we do but without sin. He caringly touched people with leprosy, healed many who were sick, fed the hungry, and faced up to people who lied to him, were opposed to him and hated him. In his ministry, Jesus gradually overcame each of those challenges in the same way we can, by prayer and relying on God our Father.

As the Son of Man, Jesus shows us he understands what we go through, and because he was victorious over sin, he can help us. In Hebrews 4:15-16, we read: 'This High Priest of ours understands our weaknesses, for he faced all of the same testings we do, yet he did not sin. So let us come boldly to the throne of our gracious God. There we will receive his mercy, and we will find grace to help us when we need it most.'

By being crucified on the Cross, the Lord Jesus also fulfilled his Father's plan to become the suffering servant described in Isaiah. This is a long passage, but it is worth reading carefully. Isaiah 53:1-5 says:

'Who has believed our message?
To whom has the Lord revealed his powerful arm?
My servant grew up in the Lord's presence like a tender green shoot,
like a root in dry ground.
There was nothing beautiful or majestic about his appearance,
nothing to attract us to him.
He was despised and rejected –
a man of sorrows, acquainted with deepest grief.
We turned our backs on him and looked the other way.
He was despised, and we did not care.

Yet it was our weaknesses he carried;
it was our sorrows that weighed him down.
And we thought his troubles were a punishment from God,
a punishment for his own sins!
But he was pierced for our rebellion,
crushed for our sins.
He was beaten so we could be whole.
He was whipped so we could be healed.'

In shedding his blood for us at the Cross, Jesus offered himself as a sacrifice for the sins of the world. Because he was fully human and died for us, we can be forgiven.

When Jesus began his ministry, he was first baptised by John the Baptist in the river Jordan. Because he was sinless, Jesus didn't need to be baptised but did so to show he was accepting God's plan to save us. The river Jordan symbolised salvation because the people of Israel had been saved from the Egyptians by escaping through the Red Sea.

Afterwards, Jesus was tempted three times in the wilderness by Satan. In each of the temptations, Satan was trying to get Jesus to use his power like a superhero. Instead, Jesus chose the path of suffering and service before him and trusted in his Father. If the Lord Jesus had given in to those temptations, God's plan of salvation for the world would have been ruined.

As a human, Jesus also had to live under the law of Moses as we read in Galatians 4:4-5: 'But when the right time came, God sent his Son, born of a woman, subject to the law. God sent him to buy freedom for us who were slaves to the law, so that he could adopt us as his very own children.' By living a completely sinless life, Jesus was able to be a perfect sacrifice for sin. This meant we could be redeemed or bought back to become God's children.

2 Corinthians 5:21 says: 'For God made Christ, who never sinned, to be the offering for our sin, so that we could be made right with God through Christ.' Jesus took our sins, and in exchange, we receive his righteousness.

In his life on earth, Jesus also fulfilled many prophecies about his birth, upbringing and death to prove he was the Messiah. It is very important to believe that the Lord Jesus came in human form. 1 John 4:2-3a reads: 'This is how we know if they have the Spirit of God: If a person claiming to be a prophet acknowledges that Jesus Christ came in a real body, that person has the Spirit of God. But if someone claims to be a prophet and does not acknowledge the truth about Jesus, that person is not from God.' Unless the Lord Jesus had become fully human, he couldn't have been a sacrifice for our sins to make us right with God.

Further reading: John 8:1-11; John 13:1-15; John 21:1-8

Growing in Jesus

✏️ To answer

1. Jesus mostly spoke about himself as the Son of _____ .

2. When the Lord Jesus takes away our sin, he gives us his _____ instead.

3. Jesus is the only person who has lived a _____ life.

4. When the Lord Jesus was tempted to do wrong, He _____ God for help.

5. When we have any kind of problem, we can know that Jesus _____ what we are going through.

💬 To discuss

1. Think of different superheroes you know something about. In what ways is Jesus like a superhero? In what ways is he different?

2. In New Testament times, people who had leprosy weren't allowed to live in villages with their families unless they could show that they were cured of the disease. How do you think the leper felt when Jesus showed compassion toward him in Matthew 8:1-4?

3. Is there someone in need that God might want you to serve in a practical way?

▶️ To do

As a family, think of someone who might be in need – perhaps they are lonely or unable to do something for themselves because of illness. Plan a way to serve them together using the example of Jesus – maybe make a meal, mow their lawns or visit them. Talk together about how God understands our needs and helps us to understand the needs of others.

🙏 Prayer

Our Heavenly Father and our God, thank you that Jesus came to live among us, that he showed us your love and care and was without fault. Help us to become more like him and to show others your love. Amen.

Week 19

What is the love of God like?

John 3:16: 'For *this is how God loved* the world: He gave his one and only Son, so that everyone who believes in him will not perish but have eternal life.'

When I was ten years old, Bible in Schools was a regular part of our learning at school. That year, Mr Hudson visited our class, taught us about Jesus, and gave us all a copy of the Bible. Mr Hudson also taught us to memorise John 3:16. Seven years later, it came back to mind when new friends at high school told me that a Christian was someone who had a personal relationship with God through Jesus. For months, the words of John 3:16 kept going around and around in my mind.

John 3:16 is perhaps the most well-known verse in the Bible, but let's break it down and explore its meaning over the following weeks. First, the phrase 'this is how God loved'. We can't see God or talk to him face to face, so we must figure out what God is like in other ways. We can look at creation and read about him in the Bible, and can study the life of Jesus, who came to earth to reveal God to us. Hearing about the change that has happened in someone's life who has come to faith in Jesus can also help us.

At high school, when I heard about Jesus, I felt strongly drawn to God because I remembered what John 3:16 told me about his love. I felt deeply in my heart and mind that God was real and that he knew me as an individual. I understood that if I was the only person on earth, Jesus would still have gone to the Cross and died on my behalf.

I was brought up in a home where we were well-clothed and fed but weren't told we were loved, so when I heard about God's love and saw it in Christian friends, it meant a lot. I realised he knew me as an individual and wanted me to have a personal relationship with him. Over several months, I gradually came to understand God knew about me and loved me. There are many aspects to God's character, but his love is the deepest and strongest part of his personality.

We hear messages about love all around us. We hear about romantic love in music, TV programmes or novels. We use expressions of love to one another in our families. We say we love our pets. We love playing sport or going to special places on holiday. We even love some of our possessions, which is weird because we can't have a relationship with them, and they can't love us back! If we are honest, we also find it easier to love others who are our friends and who are nice to us. We aren't so good at loving people who don't treat us well.

So, how is God's love different from ours?

Most of all, God's love is shown in what Jesus taught and how he gave to others during his earthly ministry. The Apostle Peter said in Acts 10:38b: 'Then Jesus went around doing good and healing all who were oppressed by the devil, for God was with him.' Jesus spent most of his time with the outcasts of society and with those who were sick. There are dozens of stories in the Gospels of people whom he healed. Jesus often went out of his way to help them and ignored his own needs for rest or even food. His love was also shown in the reassurance of forgiveness he gave to people who came to him.

For example, in Luke 5, Jesus first forgave the paralysed man who had been lowered through the roof by friends. Then he healed the man, who was then able to pick up his bed and carry it away. The writers of the Gospels gave a lot of detail about some of the healings Jesus performed because they wanted us to understand God's care and power to save us.

At present, there are just over eight billion people in the world, which might make us feel a little insignificant, but the love of God is unlimited for each individual. We don't get less of God's love just because someone near us also experiences it. God doesn't have favourites, either.

Growing in Jesus

Romans 5:5 describes God's love wonderfully: 'And this hope will not lead to disappointment. For we know how dearly God loves us, because he has given us the Holy Spirit to fill our hearts with his love.' In John 13:1b, we read that when he was preparing to go to the Cross, Jesus 'had loved his disciples during his ministry on earth, and now he loved them to the very end.'

The Apostle John was one of Jesus' closest followers. Near the end of his life, in his 80s or 90s, John wrote in 1 John 4:8 simply that: 'God is love'. John had been a disciple of the Lord Jesus throughout his ministry on earth and had many more years to learn what God was really like. 'God is love' is the most important part of God's nature to be reminded of and experience for ourselves. It changed my life and will do the same for anyone who comes to know Jesus and grow in him.

Further reading: 1 John 4:7-21; 1 Corinthians 13:7

What is the love of God like? (Week 19)

✏️ To answer

1. The basic nature of God is _ _ _ _ .

2. God didn't just keep his love up in heaven. How did he show it to us?

3. Does God ever stop loving us?

💬 To discuss

1. In what ways did Jesus show love to his disciples over the three years while he trained them?

2. How does it make you feel to know that God's love for you never fails or changes?

3. What is one way you can show love to God in return?

▶️ To do

Fold a piece of card twice to make three equal sections. Cut out a heart to represent the love of God in each section, then cover the heart-shaped spaces with coloured tissue paper or cellophane. Tape the ends of the card together to make a triangular prism, then stand it up. Place a battery-powered tea candle inside the triangle. Test each other on learning John 3:16 as a memory verse.

🙏 Prayer

Our Heavenly Father and our God, we are amazed and humbled by your love. Thank you that you don't wait for us to be good enough to join your family because Jesus makes us right with you. Amen.

Week 20

Why did God have to give his Son for us?

John 3:16: 'For this is how God loved the world: *He gave his one and only Son*, so that everyone who believes in him will not perish but have eternal life.'

A book that has greatly impacted my life is *Miracle on the River Kwai* by Ernest Gordon. It tells the story of Allied prisoners of war who the Japanese forced to build a railway in Burma in terrible conditions during World War Two. Many prisoners died under the harsh conditions or were executed for minor offences. After some time, they became less human and fought among themselves for what was needed for survival.

One day, a prisoner who was a Christian heroically took the place of a man who was about to be executed, resulting in him being beaten to death by the guards. His selfless action led to a few prisoners deciding to read the New Testament together. Gradually, instead of just thinking of their own needs, the prisoners began to follow the teachings of Jesus and care for one another. They set up a bush hospital and began to risk their lives sneaking out of the camp to get extra food for the sick.

Step by step their lives were transformed, and ultimately, they were able to show that good won over evil. When they were released at the end of the war, they were even able to forgive their Japanese guards for the terrible treatment they had experienced. Afterwards, Ernest Gordon went into Christian ministry to serve others.

You might have heard of the story about ants by the evangelist, Billy Graham. As a young boy, he was fascinated by them and spent hours watching them. He also knew that a pest exterminator would come and spray to kill the ants every month. Billy Graham asked his mother how he could warn them since they wouldn't understand his words. His mother explained to Billy that the only way to do this would be for him to become an ant himself, and then they would understand his warnings.

God did that for us by giving his Son, who gave up all his power and rights as God's Son to live among us. He gave all so we could be saved and become part of God's family.

In 1 John 4:9-10, we read this: 'God showed how much he loved us by sending his one and only Son into the world so that we might have eternal life through him. This is real love – not that we loved God, but that he loved us and sent his Son as a sacrifice to take away our sins.' God didn't just feel love toward us. He did something about it by sending Jesus to pay for our sins.

Imagine you hit a cricket ball through a window of your parent's glasshouse while you are playing cricket where you had been told not to. Your father is cross at what you have done and says you must work to pay for the repair, but before you can do that, one of your friends takes money out of their pocket and pays for the window. Your friend's gift satisfies your father's anger toward you. God feels anger at sin and injustice, and one day he will judge all wrongdoers, but God's anger is very different from ours. Psalm 103:8 says: 'The Lord is compassionate and merciful, slow to get angry and filled with unfailing love.' God is slow to anger, and he never loses his temper.

The test that love is real is that it is prepared to give to another person without expecting anything back. Much of what we hear about love through music or movies is selfish and focused on what a person can get out of a relationship rather than what they can give. Romans 5:6,8 tells us that love from God is always giving, even when it is undeserved: 'When we were utterly helpless, Christ came at just the right time and died for us sinners. God showed his great love for us by sending Christ to die for us while we were still sinners.'

We may ask questions about suffering and feel that our life is harder than that of others. One thing we can never have any doubt about is that God has shown his love for us in a way that cost him the most precious thing he had – the life of his Son. John 15:13 tells us: 'There is no greater love than to lay down one's life for one's friends.' If we know that God loved us enough to die for us, then we can trust him to help us in every difficulty we face.

Before I came to faith, I had questions about the fairness of God in telling Abraham to offer his son, Isaac, as a sacrifice. It helped me realise that even if Abraham had gone ahead and killed Isaac, God would have raised him from the dead. Abraham trusted God, proving his faith, and at the same time he learned that God was different from the false gods in the cultures around him who required human sacrifice to please them.

When we experience his love, God also calls us to live in the same way that he showed us by giving Jesus. He calls us to show love by our actions. That was the lesson learned by the Allied prisoners in Burma as God's love spread out among them and overcame the hate and cruel treatment they were shown.

Further reading: Luke 6:27-38; 1 John 2:2

Why did God have to give his Son for us? (Week 20)

✏️ To answer

1. Unscramble the words in this sentence: The way that God showed his love for us was in giving us sejsu.

2. Evil can be overcome by _ _ _ _ .

3. Even if we do _ _ _ _ _ God still loves us.

4. What is one way we can show love to others?

5. Jesus died on the _ _ _ _ _ for us even when we didn't deserve it.

💬 To discuss

1. Debate whether love always must be shown in a practical way to be real.

2. What are three ways Jesus' death on the Cross shows us God's love?

3. How can you show God your gratitude from what Jesus taught in Luke 17:11-19?

▶️ To do

Ernest Gordon and the soldiers made many things using bamboo, including medical equipment. Use some bamboo or coconut shell to make windchimes. Talk together about a time you can remember when good overcame evil.

🙏 Prayer

Our Heavenly Father and our God, thank you for showing us that good overcomes evil because it comes from you. Please give us courage to do good when we are given the opportunity. For your glory. Amen.

Week 21

What does it mean for us to believe?

John 3:16: 'For this is how God loved the world: He gave his one and only Son, so that *everyone who believes* in him will not perish but have eternal life.'

When I was at university in Christchurch, I joined the Christian Union. One very cold weekend, we had a winter camp near the Māori Lakes (Ōtūwharekai) in North Canterbury. These small lakes are quite shallow and were frozen over at the time. A few of us tested the ice and found we could walk right across one of the lakes. This probably wasn't wise so I don't recommend trying it yourself!

Jesus' invitation to believe in him is similar to this. Believing in the Lord Jesus doesn't mean just agreeing with an idea that doesn't affect our daily lives, like saying Mount Everest is the tallest mountain on the planet. Believing in Jesus means we will trust him for the forgiveness of our sins and commit our lives to him – like we did when we stepped out on the ice.

With the guidance of the Bible, the help of God's Spirit and fellow Christians, we will promise to obey him in the way he tells us to live. We will also trust him to guide us in the decisions of life. Although our group couldn't see the thickness of the ice on the lake and took a bit of a risk, what we learn about the life, death and resurrection of Jesus does give us a solid basis for believing in him.

In Mark 1:14-15, we read: 'Later on, after John was arrested, Jesus went into Galilee, where he preached God's Good News. "The time promised by God has come at last!" he announced. "The Kingdom of God is near! Repent of your sins and believe the Good News!"' As he preached,

Jesus linked the act of believing with something called repentance, which means a complete heart change and beginning to live differently.

He also said we would need to give our first loyalty to the new Kingdom of God he was teaching about. This new kingdom would set us free and, in the end, would right all the wrongs that are part of this life. Finally, he said this choice to believe that he calls us to make is wonderfully good news, which is what the word 'gospel' means!

So, believing means we need to turn from going our own way and begin to follow God's different way. In Jesus' time, people showed this by being publicly baptised, usually in a river. That was a way of showing to God and others that their newfound faith was real.

Another important thing about the gospel or good news is that Jesus' invitation to believe is offered to every single person. In 1 Timothy 2:4, we read that God 'wants everyone to be saved and to understand the truth.' The Christian writer, C.S. Lewis, says of Jesus: 'He died not for men, but for each man. If each man had been the only man made, he would have done no less.'

Have you ever met and spoken with someone who really listened to you so you felt you were the sole focus of their attention? God is like that. Although he knows every person who has lived, is living now, and will exist in the future, he also knows each one of us fully as individuals. He knows your name and knows everything about you. How we respond to God affects our experience of his love, but there is no limit to his love for us.

If you choose to believe in the Lord Jesus, you will receive new life. A little before the verse we have been concentrating on in John 3:16, Jesus had a visit from a very educated ruler of the Jews called Nicodemus. He came to talk with Jesus because he recognised that Jesus had come from God, and so Jesus began to explain to Nicodemus about the gospel and having new life.

Here's what Jesus said to Nicodemus in John 3:3-8. 'Jesus replied, "I tell you the truth, unless you are born again, you cannot see the Kingdom of God." "What do you mean?" exclaimed Nicodemus. "How can an old man go back into his mother's womb and be born again?" Jesus replied, "I assure you, no one can enter the Kingdom of God without being born of water and the Spirit. Humans can reproduce only human life, but the Holy Spirit gives birth to spiritual life. So don't be surprised when I say, 'You must be born again.' The wind blows wherever it wants. Just as you can hear the wind but can't tell where it comes from or where it is going, so you can't explain how people are born of the Spirit.'"

That's quite a complicated conversation! Nicodemus was a pretty important person. He was in the strict group of the Pharisees and was a leading teacher in Israel. What Jesus was saying to him, however, was that no matter how far he had come in life, Nicodemus needed to start again in a new life to be right with God. Nicodemus needed to be born again, and so do we. No matter how good any of us are, we can never be good enough by our own efforts. No matter how old or young we are, we need to start a new life.

When we repent and believe in the Lord Jesus, God's Spirit enters our hearts, and we experience a wonderful new life.

Further reading: 1 Peter 1:1-5; Mark 9:14-27

What does it mean for us to believe? (Week 21)

✏️ To answer

Complete the missing words:

1. God loves _ _ _ _ _ _ _ _ .

2. Jesus said to Nicodemus that he needed to be _ _ _ _ again.

3. The gospel Jesus talked about means _ _ _ _ news.

4. The word 'repent' means to turn around and follow Jesus' _ _ _ .

5. God wants to give us all _ _ _ life.

💬 To discuss

1. Why do you think Nicodemus wanted to talk to Jesus, even though he was highly educated?

2. How does it make you feel knowing Jesus would have died if you were the only person on earth?

3. Is there an area in your life where you feel Jesus wants you to trust him this week?

▶️ To do

Freeze some water in a large container like an oven dish until there is a layer of ice on top. Carefully see how much weight can you put on the ice before it breaks. Talk together about how it can be scary sometimes to trust God but how he doesn't let us down.

🙏 Prayer

Our Heavenly Father and our God, thank you that you invite us to have a new life in you because of Jesus. Please help us to place our trust in you always, knowing that you promise to never let us down. Amen.

Week 22

What is eternal life and when does it start?

John 3:16: 'For this is how God loved the world: He gave his one and only Son, so that everyone who believes in him will not perish but have *eternal life*.'

Just at the end of the COVID-19 lockdown in New Zealand, we had the sad task of taking our much-loved border terrier Ghillie to the vet. He had been diagnosed with a brain tumour and we were told we would need to have him put to sleep. So that evening we had to say goodbye to him, and then a few weeks later, we scattered his ashes at one of his favourite places at the beach.

The Bible doesn't say whether we will see our pets again in heaven, but we like to think he will be up there happily playing games of chasing. What the Bible is sure about, however, is that when we have a relationship with the Lord Jesus, we will live with him and our fellow believers forever.

Eternal life is hard to imagine because we live in a world ruled by time. We must get up in time to get to school or work and we follow a calendar of 365 days each year, followed by another year and so on. What has happened on the earth from the start of creation until the end can be measured by time, but God lives in eternity beyond time. So, time cannot measure what has happened before creation, and it can't measure what will go on after a new heaven and earth has been made as promised in the Bible.

We could try to draw a picture of it all something like this:

ETERNITY BEFORE ... [time, history] *... ETERNITY AFTERWARDS*

The Bible says that eternal life is about more than just ideas like these, however. In John 17:3, Jesus said: 'And this is eternal life, that they know you, the only true God, and Jesus Christ whom you have sent.' Eternal life is about a relationship with God through Jesus.

When Jesus was twelve, his parents made one of their annual trips to Jerusalem to celebrate the Passover feast. From their hometown in Nazareth, it was a journey of around 150km, which probably took them about a week each way. This year after the feast, as they were journeying home, they found that Jesus was missing from the group they were travelling with. After a three-day search, they found him still in Jerusalem, in the temple having a discussion with the religious teachers. The explanation he gave them was: '"But why did you need to search?" he asked. "Didn't you know that I must be in my Father's house?"' (Luke 2:49).

Jesus had found out who his Heavenly Father was and was beginning to find his purpose in life.

In John 1:12, we read: 'But to all who believed him and accepted him, he gave the right to become children of God.' Through what the Lord Jesus has done for us on the Cross, we can also have a relationship with the same Heavenly Father. So, the meaning of life for each of us, regardless of our age, is first about who we belong to, rather than what we are to do or where we go. We don't have to wait until we get to heaven to have eternal life. It starts when we believe – when God's Spirit comes into our lives and makes us alive.

The Bible tells us that when we receive Christ and are reborn to a new life, God's Spirit unites with our spirit and makes us spiritually alive. In Romans 8:15b-16, we read: 'So you have not received a spirit that makes you fearful slaves. Instead, you received God's Spirit when he adopted you as his own children. Now we call him, "Abba, Father." For his Spirit joins with our spirit to affirm that we are God's children.'

Over 20 years after Jesus was in Jerusalem as a 12-year-old, he travelled there again for the Passover feast, and while he was there, he made this promise in John 7:37-39a: 'On the last day, the climax of the festival, Jesus stood and shouted to the crowds, "Anyone who is thirsty may come to me! Anyone who believes in me may come and drink! For the Scriptures declare, Rivers of living water will flow from his heart."' Eternal life is not just about our future.

The Lord Jesus promises that if we come to him, we will experience a relationship with him that meets the innermost needs of our hearts as we grow to trust him more and more.

Eternal life is a definite promise from God, so much so that he writes our name in a special book. In Philippians 4:3, the Apostle Paul talks about his fellow Christians 'whose names are written in the Book of Life'. Further, we read in Revelation 2:17 that God gives us a new name and writes it on a white stone. The colour white symbolises victory over sin and trials and the promised new name is what we become known for as Christ forms his character in our lives.

Psychologists say that humankind's biggest fear is the fear of death. Apart from those who will still be alive when Christ returns, we will all die physically one day. But for the Christian, death has quite a different meaning. 1 Corinthians 15:55 tells us:

'O death, where is your victory?
O death, where is your sting?'

This promise of eternal life gives us something to eagerly look forward to and if we are following Jesus, it has already started.

Further reading: Romans 6:23; Hebrews 5:9

What is eternal life and when does it start? (Week 22)

✏️ To answer

Join these sentence ends to the right beginnings:

Eternal life starts from…	…back to God.
God's Spirit helps us understand…	…when God becomes our Father.
Jesus came to bring people…	…God's spirit comes into our heart.
When we believe in Jesus…	…the Bible.
God promises to give us…	…a new name.

💬 To discuss

1. The Bible tells us in 1 John 5:11-12: 'And this is what God has testified: He has given us eternal life, and this life is in his Son. Whoever has the Son has life; whoever does not have God's Son does not have life.' How do you know you have eternal life?

2. As a 12-year-old, Jesus was starting to understand God's purpose for his life. How does it make you think or feel knowing that God has a purpose for your life too?

3. Is there a way God is wanting to form the character of Jesus in your life now?

▶️ To do

Cut a piece of A4 paper longways to make two strips. Join them together to make one long strip. Draw pictures to make a timeline of your life (imagine the rest) and a blue line around it to represent eternal life. Join the ends to make a crown that fits your head. Talk together about why being with God forever could never be boring.

Growing in Jesus

 **Prayer**

Our Heavenly Father and our God, thank you that when we give you our hearts and lives you make us new. Help us to become more like Jesus each day that we might live with you forever. In his name we ask this. Amen.

Week 23

What did Jesus mean when he talked about repentance?

Have you ever experienced the feeling that roads and familiar places look very different when travelling them in a different direction? While living in Chiang Mai in Thailand, my son and I drove a dinner guest home to where they were staying in an unfamiliar part of the city. When we turned around to drive home, however, we became badly lost. Several hours later, we were still going around and around the same roads and weren't any closer to home.

After running out of other ideas, we turned in the opposite direction to where we thought we should be going, and to our relief, straight away found the main road back home.

When Jesus began his ministry, his message started with the word 'repent'. We read in Matthew 4:17: 'From then on Jesus began to preach, "Repent of your sins and turn to God, for the Kingdom of Heaven is near"'. The same message of repentance to be right with God was also preached by Jesus's cousin, John the Baptist, whose ministry was to prepare people's hearts to respond to Jesus. 'Repent' isn't a word we use much now and is quite a confronting word. Jesus used it, however, so it is important we understand what it means.

So, what does repentance mean? In the Old Testament the word was used to mean wholeheartedly returning to God from a life of sin. John required his hearers to show their repentance by confessing their sins to God and being baptised in a public place. He also talked to them very practically about the changes that should be seen in their lives from then on.

In the New Testament, the word repentance refers to a change of mind. It is important to realise that this is not just a change of how we think about our choices. It is also a deep change that affects our attitudes and priorities, how we treat other people, our overall direction in life, and our daily lifestyle. The teaching Jesus gave in the Sermon on the Mount gives us several ways this should work out in our lives.

After Jesus ascended to heaven, the first sermon preached was by the Apostle Peter in Acts 2. Peter explained what the outpouring of the Spirit his hearers had just witnessed really meant. They had heard a rushing wind and God's praises spoken about by the apostles in languages they had never learned. Peter explained this and told the people that Jesus was God's Son who had been raised from the dead. He also described their part in Jesus being killed on the Cross. Peter said that because of Jesus' sinless life and death, God had made Jesus their Saviour as well as the Lord of all who lived.

The people were deeply convicted of their sin and asked what they should do in response. Peter instructed them to repent and be baptised and then they would also receive the promised Holy Spirit.

So, repentance is not just a turning away from one way of living but a commitment to a new one. Repentance is not something God calls us to do because he is a stern, fault-finding God. It is quite the opposite. God knows, in his love, that there is nothing better for us to do than to turn from our independent, sinful way of living and to follow him with all our hearts. When God shows us our sin, he does so in love and for our good. We may start following Christ through his love shown to us in some way – by friendship or experiencing healing, but we cannot go much further without repentance.

Before I came to know Christ, I had a very foul mouth, which at the time I didn't think was a problem. One day, a Christian friend said he wished I wouldn't take Christ's name in vain. I felt so bad that I stopped blaspheming immediately. When I came to faith soon afterwards, I stopped saying other swear words, but I still had a very sarcastic tongue. It took me some time to gradually learn that what I thought was humour was hurting others.

As time went on, God taught me to use positive and encouraging words to build others up. God works in our lives in stages like this, dealing with obvious sins first. Then he helps us change the thinking and attitudes underneath so his character and love show through our lives. Repentance is turning away from one way of living and toward another one.

Regular repentance should be part of our continuing life as Christians because, as James says, we all make many mistakes (James 3:2) and, as John says, none of us are without sin (1 John 1:8). We are all a work in progress! During his ministry to the Corinthian church, Paul sometimes had to speak to them strongly for some of their behaviour. When he wrote later, however, he was able to rejoice and commend them that they had become sorry enough to repent.

God's desire for us is that we avoid the kinds of sinful choices that will cause us and others sorrow in the long run. True repentance doesn't bring sadness because repentance brings forgiveness and restoration to fellowship with God and others.

Further reading: Read the Sermon on the Mount in either Matthew 5-7 or Luke 6:20-49; 2 Corinthians 7:10

Growing in Jesus

To answer

Read the story about Zacchaeus in Luke 19:1-10 then put these parts of the story in the correct order:

Jesus tells Zacchaeus he has been saved.
Jesus tells Zacchaeus he will stay at his house.
Zacchaeus is sorry for cheating people.
People in the crowd say Jesus shouldn't be a friend to Zacchaeus.
Zacchaeus hears about Jesus.
Zacchaeus gives half his money to the poor.
Zacchaeus climbs a tree.

To discuss

1. How does repentance change a person's life?

2. Repentance is turning back toward God, who loves us and only wants our best. What are the benefits of repentance?

3. Is there an area of your life that God wants you to change in at the moment? How can you experience his help to do that?

To do

Luke 19:1-10 tells the story of Zacchaeus, who repented. Act the story out as a family. As it ends with a meal at Zacchaeus's home, you might like to do it just before you eat together.

Characters: Zacchaeus, Jesus, grumpy member of the crowd, poor person who had been cheated.

Props: something to climb on as a tree, meal table, coins.

Clothing: robes, headwear, sandals.

Talk together about what you learned by acting out this story.

What did Jesus mean when he talked about repentance? (Week 23)

 **Prayer**

Our Heavenly Father and our God, help us to turn away in our hearts and minds from anything your Word shows us is wrong. Help us to grow to become more like Jesus each day that we might glorify you. In his name we ask this. Amen.

If you have never prayed to commit your life to Jesus, then you might like to use this prayer:

Loving and Almighty God, I believe you sent the Lord Jesus to die for me and that you raised him from the dead. I confess where I have sinned against you in my thoughts, words and actions and I humbly turn away from those things. I thank you for forgiving my sins and ask that you come into my life as my Saviour and Lord. I want to follow you from now on. Please send your Holy Spirit to fill my heart and help me to follow you faithfully with my fellow believers in your church. Amen.

Week 24

What happened when the Lord Jesus rose from the dead?

Although the average life expectancy in New Zealand has gone up by over 30 years during the last century, medical science still can't prevent all of us from dying eventually. The resurrection of Jesus Christ from the dead, however, has proven that death can be overcome. Jesus' resurrection has changed more lives than anything else. Why?

After teaching and healing people for over three years, Jesus went to Jerusalem, where he knew death awaited him. Opposition and lies from the Pharisees and religious rulers led to his arrest, and then he was sentenced to death by Pilate, the Roman governor. Jesus was crucified on a cross alongside two others and hung on the cross for about six hours before giving up his spirit and dying. One of Jesus' followers, a rich man named Joseph of Arimathea, was given permission from Pilate to take Jesus' body down and bury it in his own tomb.

The Pharisees and rulers remembered that Jesus had said that he would rise from death after three days and set a guard at the entrance to the tomb. This was out of fear that Jesus' disciples would steal his body and spread a rumour that he had risen as he had promised. Although they didn't believe that, the Pharisees and rulers didn't want the problems Jesus' popularity had caused them to happen again.

The events after Jesus' resurrection went much like this. On the third day, an earthquake occurred as angels came from heaven and rolled away the stone in front of the tomb. The guards passed out from fright and the angel told Mary Magdalene, Mary the mother of James, and Salome to go and tell the disciples of Jesus' resurrection. Jesus appeared to one of the

Marys to comfort her in her grief. Peter and John then ran to the tomb and found it empty as the women had described. The eleven disciples later met with Jesus in Jerusalem and were sent to Galilee.

Jesus also appeared to two other disciples who were walking from Jerusalem to the nearby village of Emmaus. They ran back to Jerusalem and told the eleven disciples what had happened. Jesus appeared to the disciples again (less Thomas) and showed them evidence that he was alive. A week or so later, Jesus was with them again – including Thomas this time. Jesus later appeared to the eleven disciples while fishing on Lake Galilee.

Jesus later also appeared to Saul of Tarsus, who was persecuting the disciples after the stoning of Stephen. Altogether Jesus' appearances continued for 40 days after his resurrection. As well as showing his victory over death, Jesus also continued to teach his disciples. And then Jesus appeared to 500 of his followers at once and to his half-brother James. Before Jesus was crucified, James and his other brothers didn't believe in him, but James later became the leader of the church in Jerusalem and was killed for his faith.

Several miracles were also associated with Jesus' resurrection; for example, further earthquakes, and saints who had died appearing to people. Finally, at the end of the 40 days, Jesus led his disciples up to the Mount of Olives where he disappeared into heaven. The disciples returned to Jerusalem as they had been commanded and prayed until the outpouring of the Holy Spirit on the day of Pentecost, when the work of the church began.

These appearances and the instructions that Jesus gave to his disciples convinced them of what they hadn't properly understood during their three years with him: the meaning of his death and that he had conquered death for everyone who would believe in him. This gave the eleven disciples the courage to preach in his name. They knew that though the future held suffering, death was only the doorway to the joy of eternal life with God. Those who believed in Jesus later were also able to have faith through the disciples, who were eyewitnesses of Jesus' life, death and resurrection.

So, what about us? There are no eyewitnesses left to tell us what they saw happen. What do we have on which to base our trust in God? The Apostle Paul, who was one of the eyewitnesses, says this in 1 Corinthians 15:19: 'And if our hope in Christ is only for this life, we are more to be pitied than anyone in the world.'

Paul had experienced persecution and suffering, so pointed out that if following Christ was only for this life, it was a pretty poor choice! But, because of Jesus' resurrection, we do have the promise that there is a life after this one that pays us back much, much more than any hardship we might experience or give up.

Paul goes on to say in 1 Corinthians 15:20-22: 'But in fact, Christ has been raised from the dead. He is the first of a great harvest of all who have died. So you see, just as death came into the world through a man, now the resurrection from the dead has begun through another man. Just as everyone dies because we all belong to Adam, everyone who belongs to Christ will be given new life.'

What are the logical reasons we have that Jesus is alive now? Here they are:

Christianity is unique amongst religions in being based on the life of someone who died, overcame death, and then appeared alive again.

Christianity has a 'high' view of our physical bodies, i.e., that God created them as good at the beginning in Genesis. Other religions often seek to be free of the body.

During his ministry, Jesus brought at least three people back from the dead.

Before his death, Jesus prophesied that he would be raised on the third day.

Before Jesus' resurrection, the disciples were afraid and beaten. They wouldn't have been suddenly changed and willing to suffer as they did if they hadn't experienced Jesus alive amongst them again.

What happened when the Lord Jesus rose from the dead? (Week 24)

If Jesus hadn't been raised, the Pharisees and rulers could have produced his body to stop the disciples preaching about Jesus and, of course, they didn't.

Further reading: John 11:17-27; Matthew 28:6; 1 Corinthians 15:1-8; Matthew 27:51-53

Growing in Jesus

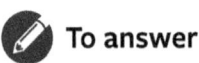 **To answer**

Choose words from the list below to finish these sentences.

1. When Jesus was crucified, the disciples were _____ .

2. When Joseph asked Pilate for Jesus' body, he was _____ .

3. When Thomas heard Jesus was alive, he was _____ .

4. When Mary recognised Jesus in the garden, she was _____ .

5. When Saul met Jesus, he was _____ .

List of words: sad, doubtful, joyful, nervous, changed.

 To discuss

1. How did the disciples' lives change when they realised Jesus had risen from the dead?

2. When Stephen was stoned to death in Acts 7:54-60, why do you think he didn't seem to be afraid?

3. What does knowing that Jesus is alive and can be with you throughout each day mean for you?

To do

Make a model of Jesus' tomb by rolling out play dough (dye it grey like rock if you can) and laying it over an upside-down bowl. Cut out a piece from the side to make the flat rock that was rolled over the entranceway. Bake in an oven for about three hours at 80° C. Talk together about what you would have felt if you were Mary meeting Jesus in the garden.

What happened when the Lord Jesus rose from the dead? (Week 24)

 **Prayer**

Our Heavenly Father and our God, we praise you that the Lord Jesus was raised back to life again! Thank you that because he is alive, we can be with you forever. Amen.

Week 25

What is powerful about the Cross?

In Mexico, there is a crater 200 kilometres wide and 20 kilometres deep, caused by the impact of the Chicxulub asteroid millions of years ago. Scientists have calculated the asteroid itself was between 10 and 15 kilometres in diameter, that 70 percent of all species on earth at the time became extinct (including the dinosaurs), and that there were worldwide tsunamis, earthquakes and volcanic eruptions as a result. Forest fires spread across the planet and dust stayed in the atmosphere for ten years.

This is undoubtedly the most powerful natural event ever to occur on planet Earth. Yet, it was tiny compared to what was achieved through the death and resurrection of Jesus Christ 2000 years ago. Through the Cross, death was turned into life and billions of lives were changed for good for eternity.

Imagine a dark road leading up to the Cross and then continuing away on the other side. On this dark road is the accumulated evil of humankind – idolatry, hate, strife, addiction, greed and exploitation of others. This is the harm done to ourselves and each other because we have broken God's commandments and chosen to live without him.

Beyond the Cross, however, the road becomes light. Hate is turned into love, strife into peace, selfishness into concern for others, and greed into giving. But this can only be achieved through Jesus Christ, and the only way for us to experience it is to go through the Cross – to make a journey from darkness into light. Within the Cross is the whole message that makes us right with God and part of his kingdom.

At the Cross, Jesus paid the price for the wrongdoings of the world, reconciled us to God and defeated the power of sin and death forever. 1 Peter 2:24 tells us: 'He personally carried our sins in his body on the Cross so that we can be dead to sin and live for what is right. By his wounds you are healed.'

To go through the Cross, we need to follow in Jesus' footsteps. We must also experience death to our old way of living – to die to self and belong to him. Paul described this in 2 Corinthians 5:15: 'He died for everyone so that those who receive his new life will no longer live for themselves. Instead, they will live for Christ, who died and was raised for them.'

For some, perhaps many, people the message of the Cross seems foolish. They prefer something more 'intellectual' or to believe in some kind of human goodness without Christ. Paul wrote in 1 Corinthians 1:17-18: 'For Christ didn't send me to baptise, but to preach the Good News – and not with clever speech, for fear that the Cross of Christ would lose its power. The message of the Cross is foolish to those who are headed for destruction! But we who are being saved know it is the very power of God.'

The message of the Cross is simple. To embrace the message of salvation through Jesus' death and resurrection requires humility to accept that God has done everything to save us from sin where we could do nothing to save ourselves. Paul goes on in 1 Corinthians 1:22-24 to say: 'It is foolish to the Jews, who ask for signs from heaven. And it is foolish to the Greeks, who seek human wisdom. So, when we preach that Christ was crucified, the Jews are offended and the Gentiles say it's all nonsense. But to those called by God to salvation, both Jews and Gentiles, Christ is the power of God and the wisdom of God.'

As well as being enormously powerful, the message of the Cross is also very costly. In Luke 9:23-24, Jesus 'said to the crowd, "If any of you wants to be my follower, you must give up your own way, take up your cross daily, and follow me. If you try to hang on to your life, you will lose it. But if you give up your life for my sake, you will save it.'

We cannot be a Christian by adding Jesus onto our lives as an extra; we must become fully his. Sometimes, there is a crisis where we must respond to his call to give him our lives and use them as he wills, no matter what. At most times, it is a day-by-day walk where we seek to honour him by making choices to put him first and serve others in several small ways.

Sometimes, Jesus' words about taking up our cross are misunderstood. Jesus wasn't referring to things we have no choice about – difficulties of one sort or another that happen as part of living in this fallen world. Rather, Jesus was saying that taking up our cross involves choosing to live for him instead of following our own will. We choose to make choices where we put God first and love others ahead of self.

Jesus' call to us to take up our cross is costly, but when we choose it we find it leads to wonderful freedom and blessing. Jesus said in Luke 6:38: 'Give, and you will receive. Your gift will return to you in full – pressed down, shaken together to make room for more, running over, and poured into your lap.' Further in 1 John 5:3 we are told: 'his commandments are not burdensome.'

Paul the Apostle had followed Jesus for many years and was a great thinker, but in Galatians 6:14, he wrote: 'As for me, may I never boast about anything except the cross of our Lord Jesus Christ. Because of that Cross, my interest in this world has been crucified, and the world's interest in me has also died.' We never get to a place where the Cross becomes any less than central in our lives.

Further reading: 1 Corinthians 1:17-24; Galatians 6:12-14; Ephesians 2:13; Philippians 2:5-11; Philippians 3:18-20; Colossians 1:19-20; Hebrews 12:2; 1 Peter 2:24

What is powerful about the Cross? (Week 25)

✏️ To answer

Finish this cloze by completing the words:

The Cross changes d_____ to l_____ and e_____ to g_____ . Because Jesus died on the Cross, we can have s_____ and be with him forever.

💬 To discuss

1. How does following the way of the Cross release God's power into people's lives?

2. How do you feel about Jesus' promise in Luke 6:38?

3. The Bible tells us in Romans 12:21 to overcome evil with good. Can you think of a situation where God might help you to make a difference by doing good?

▶️ To do

Make a harakeke (flax) cross. There are instructions on YouTube if you search 'harakeke cross'. Talk together about what the Cross means for each of you.

🙏 Prayer

Our Heavenly Father and our God, thank you for the Cross on which you gave your Son for us. It cost you everything to save us, Lord Jesus. Please help me to follow in your steps every day, knowing that you walk beside me always. Amen.

Week 26

What is special about Christian fellowship?

When my wife Linda and I were married, our pastor mentioned in his message that we might have less money but many friends. That has stuck in our minds over the last 40 years as we have been blessed with many friends. A lot of that has undoubtedly been to do with Linda's very friendly nature!

Although many of our friends are fellow believers in the Lord Jesus, others, though no less precious, aren't. We've found, however, that when we meet fellow Christians, even for the first time, there is an immediate heart and mind connection with them.

The word 'fellowship' in the Bible describes a deep connection we have as believers in Jesus from our shared faith and God's Spirit being present in our lives. Philippians 2:1 talks about the way we can have shared 'fellowship together in the Spirit,' and then in 1 John 1:3, the Apostle John longs for his readers to share the fellowship they have 'with the Father and with his Son, Jesus Christ.' So, fellowship has a vertical part with God as well as a horizontal one with each other. When we meet as Christians, we meet as part of Jesus' body, with him as our head. Our fellowship includes not just human friendship but the presence of Christ, the Holy Spirit and our Heavenly Father.

As a new Christian in my late teens, I spent a lot of time with several other guys to the point where we became known as the 'musketeers'. We fixed cars, led youth groups, tramped, rode motorbikes together and so on. Later, we were at each other's weddings, and though we lost touch a bit when our families were growing up, in recent years, we are getting together again. What drew us together when we were young wasn't so much what we did together but recognising that when we got together, God was there also. We each tried to give him first place in our lives even as our lives began to take different directions. That was especially true when we took time out to pray together.

Proverbs 27:17 says, 'As iron sharpens iron, so a friend sharpens a friend', and our times together helped us all walk with Jesus. When a knife is sharpened against steel, the steel removes the small imperfections from the blade, making it a sharp cutting edge. When we make it our practice to include the Lord Jesus in our friendships, by praying and seeking God together, our friendship becomes genuine fellowship.

Regular fellowship with other Christians is important, where we do more than just hang out together. A single stick taken out of a fire, even if it is on fire at the start, will get cold, and eventually, the flame will go out. As Hebrews 10:24-25 says: 'Let us think of ways to motivate one another to acts of love and good works. And let us not neglect our meeting together, as some people do, but encourage one another, especially now that the day of his return is drawing near.'

The Apostle John says in 1 John 1:6-7: 'So we are lying if we say we have fellowship with God but go on living in spiritual darkness; we are not practicing the truth. But if we are living in the light, as God is in the light, then we have fellowship with each other, and the blood of Jesus, his Son, cleanses us from all sin.' We each have a responsibility to help one another to become more like Jesus by the example we set.

The Lord Jesus also said about our meeting together for prayer in Matthew 18:19-20: 'I also tell you this: If two of you agree here on earth concerning anything you ask, my Father in heaven will do it for you. For where two or three gather together as my followers, I am there among them.' This doesn't mean we can just agree in our minds that God will answer whatever prayers we pray. It means God promises to bless our unity of heart and trust in Jesus together. If these two things are right, there is nothing to get in the road of God answering our prayers.

Fellowship in God can also overcome natural barriers between us, which may be there because of our different backgrounds or personalities. 1 Corinthians 12:13 says: 'Some of us are Jews, some are Gentiles, some are slaves, and some are free. But we have all been baptised into one body by one Spirit, and we all share the same Spirit.'

Fellowship can also reach out to include others in the body of Christ in very practical ways. In 2 Corinthians 8, Paul commends the Macedonian believers for their partnership or fellowship with him in sending aid to help the Christians in Judea who were suffering from a famine.

In Acts 2:42-46, the fellowship meetings of the early Christians in Jerusalem included both spiritual and practical aspects: 'All the believers devoted themselves to the apostles' teaching, and to fellowship, and to sharing in meals (including the Lord's Supper), and to prayer. A deep sense of awe came over them all, and the apostles performed many miraculous signs and wonders. And all the believers met together in one place and shared everything they had. They sold their property and possessions and shared the money with those in need. They worshipped together at the temple each day, met in homes for the Lord's Supper, and shared their meals with great joy and generosity.'

There are also several wonderful friendships in Scripture where the friends are God-focussed. We can think of Ruth and her mother-in-law, Naomi, of David and Jonathan in the Old Testament, and Paul and Timothy in the New Testament.

Further reading: Colossians 1:18; 1 Samuel 18:1-5

What is special about Christian fellowship? (Week 26)

 **To answer**

Read Ruth 1:1-17 and put these five sentences in the correct order:

Naomi and Elimelech went to Moab.
There was a famine in Israel.
Elimelech died.
Naomi's two sons died.
Ruth travelled to Israel with Naomi.

 To discuss

1. How can Christian fellowship be stronger than friendship?

2. How can you be strengthened or give strength to other Christians when you meet together?

3. Is there a Christian friend you might begin to pray with?

 To do

Collect a dozen small sticks and make sure you can break one. Try breaking all the sticks when you have tied them together. Take away one stick at a time until you break all remaining sticks. Talk together about how we can support one another as Christians.

 Prayer

Our Heavenly Father and our God, thank you for being with us in a special way when we meet with other Christians. Please help us to remember you in all our friendships. Through Jesus we pray. Amen.

Week 27

Where is the Lord Jesus now, and what is heaven like?

Imagine one day you are suddenly carried from wherever you are to the middle of a huge, dimly lit room about the size of a school gymnasium.

Looking around, you can't see any furniture or other objects nearby nor where the dim light comes from. Because it's hard to see, you don't want to walk around and bump into anything. But as your eyes begin to adjust, you notice there seems to be a picture of some sort on the wall at one end of the room.

You walk slowly toward the picture to see what you can make out. As you get nearer, you are surprised to see scenes from your own life painted there. Your eyes are drawn to one end of the wall where you see yourself as a small child and the picture is of your very earliest memory. Spread along the wall, you see other pictures showing you a little older – pre-school, primary school, then becoming a teenager.

As you look at the various scenes and remember your childhood, you realise each scene represents a particularly happy event in your memory. You see a party, a favourite childhood toy, a best friend, a special family holiday. Each shows a memory that stands out because of its happiness or sense of contentment or achievement. Right toward the end of the wall are the most recent scenes, where the memories are still fresh in your mind. All these scenes are very happy ones – the whole wall reads like a highlights reel of your life.

As you study the last parts of the picture near the far end from where you started, you realise the dim light in the room has been coming through a small hole. The hole is about finger-sized and is in the wall near where you're standing. As you look toward the hole, the light coming through seems to grow brighter and brighter. Strangely, you begin to feel a sense of anticipation and joy about what you might see if you look through it. You get nearer and bend to take a look. As you look, you also hear delightful sounds and smell wonderful scents like those of a rose garden mixed in with blossom trees.

Peering through the hole, you realise there is activity of some sort on the other side of the wall. It takes time for your eyes to adjust, but you make out people and hear sounds unlike any you have seen or heard before. Wonderful scenes become visible, and you are awestruck by the beauty and brightness.

Even though the painted pictures on the wall of the room you are in are of your happiest memories, your heart beats faster as you realise that what you see on the other side of the wall is so much better and makes even your happiest memories seem dull. You realise there is another whole world you have never been aware of, and the wonder and beauty of that world is so much better than anything you could have dreamed of or hoped to experience in your life.

While you keep looking, a desire grows in your heart to be in that other world – to live there so that you can fully experience what you see. The desire becomes stronger and stronger until you can't think of anything else.

Suddenly, the scenes and figures on the other side of the wall move aside, and your attention is drawn to a man approaching in shining white clothing. He becomes larger and larger as he draws near. Everything about him gives off light, and though the light hurts your eyes a bit, you realise that the light that comes from him is what's giving life and beauty to everything around him. You feel your whole heart and mind being drawn to him in love. You realise that your desire to live in this wonderful place outside the dim room is a desire to be with him and love him forever...

———

This story is an allegory to describe heaven. Like all allegories, it can only tell part of a story.

Jesus talked about heaven in John 14:2: 'There is more than enough room in my Father's home. If this were not so, would I have told you that I am going to prepare a place for you?' In 1 Corinthians 2:9, Paul's words read: 'That is what the Scriptures mean when they say, "No eye has seen, no ear has heard, and no mind has imagined what God has prepared for those who love him."'

Paul had visited heaven, but even he wasn't able to put into words what he had seen. We can be encouraged, however, that there is a special place Jesus has prepared for us and that if he has got it ready, it will be more wonderful than we could imagine. Other verses in Scripture also refer to heaven, telling us about wonderful things like worship, angels, healing, a Book of Life, everything being new, and our reigning with Jesus.

Further reading: Revelation 4:2; Matthew 25:31; 2 Peter 3:13; Revelation 21:1-5; Hebrews 11:16; Revelation 22:1-5

Where is the Lord Jesus now, and what is heaven like? (Week 27)

 **To answer**

Write an acrostic poem about HEAVEN.

 **To discuss**

1. In what ways will heaven be better than where we are now?

2. How can the promise of being in heaven with the Lord Jesus help us to follow him in this life?

3. Read Luke 12:33. How can we choose to live today to store up riches in heaven ready for when we arrive?

 **To do**

Find a shoe box and use a pencil to make a hole in one end. The inside of the box represents the room in the allegory about heaven. The outside of the box is heaven. Talk together about what objects you could put on the box to describe what heaven is like. You might like to draw some and colour them in.

 **Prayer**

Our Heavenly Father and our God, thank you that the future you have planned for us is more wonderful than we can imagine, and that the Lord Jesus is preparing a special place for us with you. Please help us to live to glorify you now. Amen.

Week 28

How do we grow as Jesus' followers?

Several years ago, we bought a Mission Fig tree. As it was winter when we picked it up, it looked just like a stick with some roots on, but the plant nursery promised us that when spring arrived, it would put out buds and grow leaves. We carefully followed all the instructions for planting it but unfortunately, it never came to life, so we pulled it out and went back to the nursery to collect a replacement.

The second tree got the same care, but it behaved like a fig tree should and put out leaves at the right time, growing new branches each year. After a year or two, it grew large, delicious figs.

In John 15, Jesus described himself as a vine and us as his branches. We read this in John 15:1-4: 'I am the true grapevine, and my Father is the gardener. He cuts off every branch of mine that doesn't produce fruit, and he prunes the branches that do bear fruit so they will produce even more. You have already been pruned and purified by the message I have given you. Remain in me, and I will remain in you. For a branch cannot produce fruit if it is severed from the vine, and you cannot be fruitful unless you remain in me.'

Jesus said the only way our lives could bear fruit was by being connected to him. Some of his hearers believed they were God's children just because they were born in Israel, attended the temple and acted in a religious way. Jesus said to them that until they turned from their sins and committed their lives to him, they couldn't call themselves God's children. The branches that were just religious, Jesus said, would be taken away.

Those of us who have chosen to follow Jesus are connected to the life of

God. God's love flows through our lives to help us bear fruit by living a life that is pleasing to him. What God wants most of all is for Jesus to be seen in our lives. When John the Baptist was talking about Jesus, he said in John 3:30: 'He must become greater and greater, and I must become less and less.' As we gradually become less selfish and more focused on Jesus, others will see more of him in our lives.

What is it that others will see? We would have been very disappointed if our fig tree, instead of producing figs, produced poisonous berries. In the same way, God wants to see the right kind of fruit in our lives. The fruits of God's Spirit are described in Galatians 5:22-23: 'But the Holy Spirit produces this kind of fruit in our lives: love, joy, peace, patience, kindness, goodness, faithfulness, gentleness, and self-control. There is no law against these things!'

This list gives us a lot to work on, but 2 Corinthians 3:18 encourages us that as we spend time with God, his Spirit helps us to change from the inside out to become more like Jesus.

As well as character qualities, by his Spirit, God has placed gifts in our lives that he helps us to develop so that we can serve him. In Hebrews 1:9, we read this about Jesus: 'You love justice and hate evil. Therefore, O God, your God has anointed you, pouring out the oil of joy on you more than on anyone else.' The 'therefore' tells us that the anointing for power on Jesus' ministry was the result of the righteousness of his life.

Because Jesus lived a life that was perfectly pleasing to his Father, he was able to accomplish all the wonderful things he did during his ministry and to keep to the path laid out before him as far as the Cross.

In Matthew 25:14-30, Jesus told the parable of the talents, where three servants were given different amounts of money to invest while their master was away. When he returned, two of them had increased the money they were entrusted, while one was afraid and buried his talent in the ground. God has given each of us talents; it doesn't matter if they are different from those of our friends or if we have less talent in a particular area.

Growing in Jesus

Eric Liddell, the Scottish runner who won a gold and a bronze medal at the 1924 Paris Olympics, said that: 'God made me fast. And when I run, I feel his pleasure.' It is right to feel God's pleasure when we are using the talents he has given us for his glory and to remember at the same time what Jesus said in John 15:5: 'for apart from me you can do nothing.'

Remember the third servant in the parable in Matthew 25:24-25 who buried his talents in the ground? When he was called to give account, he said: 'Master, I knew you were a harsh man, harvesting crops you didn't plant and gathering crops you didn't cultivate. I was afraid I would lose your money, so I hid it in the earth. Look, here is your money back.'

This servant lacked faith, which led to fear, but he also misunderstood God. He saw him as an unloving, unpredictable and unfair person. While God wants to see faith in our lives, Galatians 5:6 tells us it is God's love that motivates our faith. God is the opposite of what the third servant thought. He is just, loving and merciful.

God has given all of us who belong to him his Spirit to develop the fruits and character of Jesus in our lives. As we are connected to the life of Jesus in a love relationship, his character will steadily develop in us to God's glory and the blessing of others.

Further reading: 2 Peter 1:1-8; Romans 12:9-21; Ephesians 5:1; 1 John 2:6

How do we grow as Jesus' followers? (Week 28)

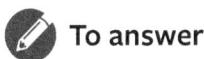 To answer

Match these lists on the fruits of the Spirit:

Love means	being right with God and others
Joy means	waiting until the right time
Peace means	keeping our word
Patience means	God's warm strength in our hearts
Kindness means	helping another person
Faithfulness means	putting God and others ahead of ourselves
Gentleness means	not losing our temper
Self-control means	being sensitive toward others

To do

There are nine fruits of God's Spirit in Galatians 5. Draw different kinds of fruit on card and write a fruit of the Spirit on each one. Join them with string and kebab skewers to make a mobile. Talk together about which of the fruits you need to work on developing with God's help.

 Prayer

Our Heavenly Father and our God, thank you that you invite us to have a relationship with you through Jesus. We want to live in him and to grow fruit that pleases you. Help us to trust you and to be your friends. Through Jesus we ask this. Amen.

Week 29

What does God say about how valuable we are?

Soon after Stephen was stoned to death in Jerusalem, as recorded in Acts 7, persecution caused many of the new believers in Jesus to move to other places. Once the persecution had quietened down, the Apostle Peter, who had stayed in Jerusalem, went to visit some of them. He was staying with Simon, a leather tanner at Joppa, a town on the coast to the west of Jerusalem. At about midday, God gave Peter a vision while he was praying on the rooftop.

Peter's vision was of many different animals that Jewish laws said he wasn't meant to eat. To his surprise, Peter heard these words three times, recorded in Acts 10:13: 'Then a voice said to him, 'Get up, Peter; kill and eat them.' Peter objected as he had been careful all life to keep this law, but to his surprise, the voice speaking then said, in verse 15: 'Do not call something unclean if God has made it clean.'

Immediately after this, some Gentile (or non-Jewish) visitors arrived, asking him to visit a Roman Centurion, Cornelius, in the town of Caesarea. Jews didn't normally have much contact with Gentiles; however, Peter understood it was God's will for him to go with them. This amazing story was the start of the gospel reaching Gentiles and not being limited to the Jews.

God was saying to Peter that the death of the Lord Jesus on the Cross provided cleansing for all people, no matter their background, culture, ethnicity or social status. No one was to be called 'unclean' or ordinary anymore. God said that no one should be looked down on because he was giving to all those who believed in him new life and a new identity in Jesus. Everyone who believed would now be accepted as his sons and daughters.

If we are believers in Jesus and have committed our lives to follow him, God says the same thing to us. We may have thought of ourselves as being common or less important to God, perhaps because of what others have said to us. Once we belong to Jesus, we can see ourselves differently as we hear God saying: 'Do not call something unclean if God has made it clean.'

Pride, which is wrong, can be thinking too much of ourselves, but it can also be thinking too little of ourselves. Either way, the most important answer to the question 'Ko wai au?' or 'Who am I?' is that we belong to God.

A few years after Peter had his vision, the Apostle Paul was writing to the Christians in Corinth. Paul pointed out to them in 1 Corinthians 1:26-27: 'Remember, dear brothers and sisters, that few of you were wise in the world's eyes or powerful or wealthy when God called you. Instead, God chose things the world considers foolish in order to shame those who think they are wise. And he chose things that are powerless to shame those who are powerful.' Paul knew that some Corinthian Christians were trying to make themselves look more important than others. Some also thought too much about outward things like knowledge and spiritual gifts rather than loving one another.

Paul reminded them of what God had given them in Jesus in 1 Corinthians 1:30: 'God has united you with Christ Jesus. For our benefit God made him to be wisdom itself. Christ made us right with God; he made us pure and holy, and he freed us from sin.' Through Jesus, God has freely given us all that really counts in life by making us right in his sight and redeeming or purchasing us back to be part of his family.

As we have seen, most of Jesus' ministry was to those whom society looked down on. These were the poor, the sick, the less educated and those struggling with sin. They were the ones who welcomed Jesus' ministry of healing and freedom and who responded to his words.

As we are growing up, we can have the same kind of feelings the people who listened to Jesus also had. In school, where we are placed with thirty or so others of the same age as ourselves, it is easy to compare. There will always be others who are better at Maths or English, who are better at sport, more confident at speaking in front of others, and so on. At school, I was good academically but was very shy and lacked ability at sport. In the two games of cricket I played, I scored zero and zero not out. At least I was improving! Just about every school report I ever received said that I lacked confidence.

If you can identify with me as a young person, perhaps these verses will be an encouragement. Psalm 56:9b says: 'This I know: God is on my side!' and Psalm 118:6 says: 'The Lord is for me, so I will have no fear. What can mere people do to me?'

We must be careful not to compare ourselves with others because very little good comes from it. In 2 Corinthians 10:12b, Paul warned the Corinthians against making comparisons, saying those who did were without understanding. A much better mindset to have is Ephesians 1:5: 'God decided in advance to adopt us into his own family by bringing us to himself through Jesus Christ. This is what he wanted to do, and it gave him great pleasure.'

In Paul's time, when a person was adopted, they became a brand-new person, just as we do when we believe in Jesus. Also, it meant that children who were adopted were able to receive their inheritance straight away. This means that when God looks at us, we have the same status as the Lord Jesus. He makes certain of this by putting his Holy Spirit in our lives.

Further reading: Ephesians 1:3-4; Romans 12:2-3; Proverbs 3:26; 2 Timothy 1:7

What does God say about how valuable we are? (Week 29)

✏️ To answer

Fill in the gaps in these sentences using these words:

family, special, others, everyone, new

1. God wants _____ to hear the good news of Jesus.
2. We are all _____ to God.
3. It is not good to compare ourselves with _____ .
4. In Jesus, God has given us _____ life.
5. God showed Peter that he wants everyone to be in his _____ .

💬 To discuss

1. Someone once said: 'There is level ground in front of the Cross'. What do you think this might mean?

2. How does knowing Jesus is with us help us when we face challenges?

3. Is there someone you know who you could give encouragement to?

▶️ To do

Sometimes, God just needs us to open the door a small amount for him to make a big difference in a situation. He multiplies what might just be a small amount of faith we have in prayer. The game of Tiddlywinks is like that – a small movement makes the disc jump a long way. Play a game of Tiddlywinks together. Talk together about a time when making a small decision led to a wonderful thing happening.

🙏 Prayer

Our Heavenly Father and our God, thank you that we are so valuable to you that you gave Jesus for us. Help us to be confident in you and your plan for our lives we ask. Through Jesus we pray. Amen.

Week 30

What will happen at the end of time when Jesus returns?

When the New Testament was written, it was difficult to be a Christian. The same Jewish leaders who had caused Jesus to be crucified were also persecuting the new believers. Some were killed by the Jews for their faith in Jesus. Many of the Gentile or non-Jewish churches were also persecuted because they now refused to worship the false gods that were popular in their cities.

There was a profitable industry in some places making idols, and some new believers had now left this industry, so they lost income as well as becoming unpopular with friends or family. Each Roman province also had a governor, who had the power of life and death, so to be a Christian in some places was dangerous.

In Acts 17, Paul and Silas arrived from Antioch to a city called Thessalonica. After preaching the gospel there, many people believed in Jesus. The Jewish leaders became very jealous of Paul and Silas and stirred up a violent mob, so Paul and Silas had to leave town. They then went to nearby Berea, but the Jewish leaders from Thessalonica followed them and caused trouble.

In 1 Thessalonians, Paul wrote to these persecuted new believers about the return of the Lord Jesus. This was to encourage them that the difficulties they were going through would one day be over and that the wrongs they were experiencing would be put right.

During Jesus' ministry, many people hoped he would announce himself as King or Messiah and bring them military deliverance from Roman rule.

Instead, Jesus came as a servant leader who would suffer to overcome the power of sin and to pay the penalty for our wrongdoing. Once Jesus had completed his mission and risen from the dead, he gave final instructions to his disciples and went up to heaven, where he is seated at the right hand of the Father. This symbolises the place of authority.

Peter announced to his hearers in Acts 2:36 that not only had Jesus died for everyone's sins, but he was Lord and Messiah. Peter was saying Jesus was now the highest authority; the King of all. Philippians 2:10-11 also makes it clear that Jesus is the highest authority over all people and that in the future, he will show his power, even over those who didn't believe in him.

The title 'Messiah' meant the one whom God would send to rescue his people. The Thessalonian Christians Paul was speaking to were suffering and rejected by society, but he promised them that one day Jesus would return from heaven to rescue them, take them to heaven, and set up his kingdom on earth where they would reign together with him.

Jesus said a lot about his return before his crucifixion and spoke about what would happen on earth before he returned. Many Christians through the years have tried to interpret current events to predict when Jesus will return. In Matthew 24:36, however, Jesus said that only the Father knows this date. He encourages us to focus on living properly for him rather than just thinking about the future.

Although we don't know when Jesus will return, we do know some things for certain. Here are the main signs, events and promises that are given in the Bible:

- The good news of the gospel will be preached to all people.
- There will be wars, famines and earthquakes in many places.
- A person or antichrist will appear; someone who opposes Jesus in every way.
- The antichrist will encourage wrong living and rebellion against God.
- There will be attacks on God's people.
- False teachers will try to lead God's people away from the truths of the Bible.

- Jesus will return suddenly, even if it isn't soon.
- Angels will help gather all believers to Jesus, and Christians who have died in the past will be raised first to meet Jesus as he returns.
- There will be judgement on those who rejected Jesus.
- Evil will end.
- Jesus will rescue the oppressed and reward the poor.
- He will establish his kingdom and make a new heaven and earth.
- We are promised we will reign with him.
- We are promised new bodies and healing from all illnesses and hurts.
- He promises to wipe away every tear we have shed and give us overwhelming joy.
- Everything will be made new again.

C.S. Lewis, the famous Christian thinker and writer, once wrote in his book, *The Great Divorce*, that when Jesus returns, God will take all our bad experiences and turn them backward into good, and that any pleasure people gained from sin would also be turned back and ruined. This idea is called 'retrograde', and interestingly, God has built it into the universe to help us understand it. For example, when we look at the planet Mars from the same point over time, it appears to move backwards.

When Christ returns and takes us to heaven with him, we will receive rewards. These will be based not just on what we have done but also on the attitude, motives and spirit with which we did those things. God will reward us for how much like Jesus we have become, how we have lived to his glory, and what blessing our lives have been to others as we have journeyed through life.

Further reading: Matthew 24:1-14; 1 John 2:18-25; 1 John 5:1-5, 18-21; 1 Corinthians 15:42-44

What will happen at the end of time when Jesus returns? (Week 30)

To answer

Find the five things that God will make new in this Word Find:

B	T	U	H	G	A
L	I	F	E	U	C
R	E	W	A	R	D
D	J	Q	L	X	J
E	A	R	T	H	O
H	M	S	H	K	Y

To discuss

1. What do you think about this statement: 'We should live like Jesus died yesterday, rose again today and is coming again tomorrow.'

2. What do you think or feel knowing God has made Jesus Lord of all people and all powers in heaven and earth?

3. Is there something you have been finding difficult that you can 'hang in there' with by knowing God is with you?

To do

Try to find the planet Mars in the night sky using a star chart from www.stardome.org.nz. The star charts are in the menus at the bottom of the home page. Next, look at a video of the Apparent Retrograde Motion of Mars on either ScienceWorld or LiveScience. Talk together about how you might look forward to a reward when you meet Jesus for having made a good choice.

Growing in Jesus

 **Prayer**

Our Heavenly Father and our God, we are excited that one day Jesus will return and take us to be with you always. Please make us strong until then to walk with you and shine your light to others. Through Jesus we pray. Amen.

Week 31

What did Jesus mean when he talked about the world?

Infrared or heat-seeking cameras are used by Search and Rescue organisations to find people lost in the bush. The cameras are mounted in helicopters or drones and can locate people who are in the bush but unable to be seen by human eye. The people show up on a screen held by the searchers.

During his ministry, Jesus often spoke with his disciples about a spiritual world that was real but unseen by their eyes. Just as an infrared camera can show people hidden under trees, so there is a spiritual world around us that we need to be aware of and guard against.

In the Bible, the word 'world' is used in several ways. First, there is the whole created world of land, sea, animals and plants that was made by God. It can also mean all the people of the world who are loved by God. Lastly, it means the invisible world system which is in rebellion against God and is controlled by Satan.

Behind the scenes of daily life, there is this unseen world system. It started when Satan led a rebellion against God and tempted Adam and Eve to sin. In doing so, Satan was successful in setting up a kingdom of darkness or a dark spiritually-based world on the earth. In John 14:30 Jesus said that Satan was the ruler of this world, and John 7:7 says that the world hated Jesus because he said what it did was evil.

Although Jesus identified Satan as the spiritual ruler of this invisible world, he also said in John 12:31 that Satan had no power over him and predicted his defeat at the Cross: 'The time for judging this world has come, when Satan, the ruler of this world, will be cast out.' With his victory at the Cross, we have Jesus' promise he would overcome evil to bring life and good to people who believed in him.

Jesus described Satan's purpose in John 10:10 to harm people and then described his own mission: 'The thief's purpose is to steal and kill and destroy. My purpose is to give them a rich and satisfying life.'

Sin from Satan's kingdom of darkness is evidenced in greed, dishonesty, violence, injustice and exploitation of the poor. In 1 John 2:15a, we are told: 'Do not love this world nor the things it offers you.' If we are believers, we should live differently to show that God has rescued us from the world and placed us in his kingdom of goodness and light. John 1:9,12 says: 'The one who is the true light, who gives light to everyone, was coming into the world. To all who believed him and accepted him, he gave the right to become children of God.'

As God's children who have been rescued from the world, we grow in Jesus so that our lives glorify him and experience the wonderful life Jesus promises. James 1:27 tells us this means caring for the needy and keeping away from sin. In Galatians 6:14, we are told this involves resisting our selfish desires to be obedient to God and losing our interest in the evil things of the world.

Not belonging to the world is a matter of our heads and hearts rather than who or where we spend our time. To obey Jesus by loving our neighbour, we need to be out among people. In John 17, Jesus prays for his followers (including us) who have left the kingdom of darkness and no longer belong to Satan's evil world system. In John 17:14-17, Jesus said: 'I have given them your word. And the world hates them because they do not belong to the world, just as I do not belong to the world. I'm not asking you to take them out of the world, but to keep them safe from the evil one. They do not belong to this world any more than I do. Make them holy by your truth; teach them your word, which is truth.'

Jesus is praying that the Father would keep his followers safe as they show and tell others about him. In Romans 12:21, we are given a command with a promise: 'Don't let evil conquer you, but conquer evil by doing good.'

Being lights in the world to proclaim the gospel won't be without difficulty, but Jesus said in John 16:33 that his death and resurrection had already won victory over the world. 1 John 5:4 says that even though we must live in the world: 'every child of God defeats this evil world, and we achieve this victory through our faith.'

The end of the Bible, in Revelation 11:15b, assures us that one day the world will be God's again, and that evil will be completely defeated forever. 'The world has now become the Kingdom of our Lord and of his Christ, and he will reign forever and ever.'

Further reading: John 15:18-19; 1 John 4:4; Acts 7:54-60

Growing in Jesus

✏️ To answer

This Word Find has three things that belong to the world and three things that belong to Jesus' Kingdom. Find them and put them into two lists.

T	Q	L	O	V	E
R	A	L	I	E	S
U	S	G	O	O	D
T	G	R	E	E	D
H	A	T	E	B	Y

💬 To discuss

1. In what ways are you aware of the influence of the world around you?

2. How does it make you think or feel knowing the Lord Jesus has already won the victory against darkness?

3. What is one way God would want his light to shine out from your life this week?

▶️ To do

Get a small photograph of yourself, a piece of cardboard, and a mirror with a straight edge. Hold a piece of card against the photograph so the edge of the card is lined up with the middle of your face. Can you see the rest of your face? Now, hold the mirror in place of the card. Why can you now see your whole face? Think about the light hitting the mirror as coming from God. Talk together about how we can shine God's light to others.

What did Jesus mean when he talked about the world? (Week 31)

 **Prayer**

Our Heavenly Father and our God, please make us wise as we live in a world that is opposed to your kingdom. Please make us strong as we grow in Jesus who is already the Lord of all. Amen.

Week 32

What is the special meaning of being in God's family, the church?

After storms, sea sponges often wash up on the beach because the waves break them off from the sea bottom. Sponges look like plants but are actually animals. Their bodies are made of a skeleton of calcium carbonate or silica with two openings. One opening allows water to enter and the second allows water to leave. A system of tubes runs between the two openings.

Sponges don't have tissues or organs, but they do have several types of cells. Some cells build the skeleton, while others produce a water current or collect food. There are also cells that glue them to the sea bottom and protect against disease. Sponges have the unique ability to regenerate their bodies again if they are broken into pieces. They can do this because all the cells know where they belong and can move back into the right place and carry on doing the same job they did before. Each cell does the job it is made for, and together, all the cells help the sponge to live, grow and reproduce.

In his letter to the Christians in Corinth, Paul also compared Christians to a spiritual body with many different parts. He wrote in 1 Corinthians 12:12: 'The human body has many parts, but the many parts make up one whole body. So it is with the body of Christ.' Paul was saying that God has made us each a part of the same body and he has given each of us a gift so we can glorify God and be of benefit to others.

One of the most obvious differences between a sea sponge and us is that our bodies have a head, and a sponge doesn't. Jesus, of course, is the head of the church. The church now represents Jesus on this earth, and we are

What is the special meaning of being in God's family, the church? (Week 32)

to carry on his work. In 1 Peter 2:4a,5a, we are told: 'You are coming to Christ, who is the living cornerstone of God's temple. And you are living stones that God is building into his spiritual temple.' God has made us and given us gifts to be a part of the church when we believe. Over time, he grows and shapes us so we can fit into the place he has planned.

As we get to know God better, he reveals to us what our place is and helps us to fulfil it. His Spirit, who comes to live in our hearts when we believe, gives gifts to each of us. In 1 Corinthians 12 Paul lists several different gifts, many of which help build others up when the church meets together. There are also other lists of gifts in places like Romans 12, Ephesians 4 and 1 Peter 4. Some of these gifts involve speaking and others are very practical, but all are important.

In 1 Corinthians 12:23, Paul said: 'And the parts we regard as less honourable are those we clothe with the greatest care.' Perhaps this might make us think of the sponge cells that glue the sponge down to the rock. They are unseen, but essential. Honouring the less-seen people is opposite from the way things often happen in the world, and we should make a real effort to honour those the world might think are less important.

Jesus showed this when he spent most of his time with the poor and less-recognised in society. There is a lovely story in Acts 9:36-42 of a woman called Tabitha, who had died. She was well-known for helping others. As the Apostle Peter prayed, she was raised to life again – perhaps because of her loving service.

Philippians 2:3-4 says: 'Don't be selfish; don't try to impress others. Be humble, thinking of others as better than yourselves. Don't look out only for your own interests, but take an interest in others, too.' It can take a lot of practice to truly let go of selfish attitudes toward others, but as we do, we know the joy of the Lord in our hearts.

As we get to know God better, his Spirit will also bring out hidden gifts we didn't think were there. Paul's advice to his young friend Timothy is worth noting. He said in 1 Timothy 4:12: 'Don't let anyone think less of you because you are young. Be an example to all believers in what you say, in the way you live, in your love, your faith, and your purity.' Later, he reminded Timothy in 2 Timothy 1:6 to: 'fan into flames the spiritual gift God gave you when I laid my hands on you.'

We shouldn't wait till we are older to start learning to serve God and others. God has things for us to do right away. Perhaps we can learn from someone who is older, as Timothy learned from Paul.

The church, then, is Jesus' body here on earth, and it is very important to meet together regularly in order to learn more about following him. Hebrews 10:24-25 says: 'Let us think of ways to motivate one another to acts of love and good works. And let us not neglect our meeting together, as some people do, but encourage one another, especially now that the day of his return is drawing near.' Being part of the church helps us care for others, and others can care for us when we go through tough times.

Later in Hebrews 13:17, we are told: 'Obey your spiritual leaders, and do what they say. Their work is to watch over your souls, and they are accountable to God. Give them reason to do this with joy and not with sorrow. That would certainly not be for your benefit.' Our parents and leaders in the church have this responsibility to teach us God's ways and to help us follow Jesus.

Further reading: Roman 12:6-8; Matthew 16:18; Ephesians 4:11-13; 1 Corinthians 12:4-11

What is the special meaning of being in God's family, the church? (Week 32)

✏️ To answer

Match these organs in the body to the job they do:

stomach	thinking
heart	tasting
brain	pumping blood
kidneys	cleaning blood
tongue	digesting

💬 To discuss

1. 'A clue to what gifts God has given us is to find out what we are good at and what we enjoy.' Do you agree or disagree with this statement?

2. Is there a gift God might be wanting to develop in your life? Who might help you identify it?

3. Is there someone God might want you to serve with a gift he has placed in your life?

▶️ To do

Find out where the different organs and bones are in the human body. Play a game of 'Simon Says' with body organs and bones. Talk together about a gift God might want you to develop to serve others.

🙏 Prayer

Our Heavenly Father and our God, thank you that you invite me to be part of your body the church. Thank you for the gifts that you give me to serve you with my brothers and sisters In Jesus. Please help me to use these for your glory. Amen.

Week 33

Why do we still do the wrong thing sometimes?

The Christian life is full of unexpected opposites – Jesus died then was raised to life, we are told to love our enemies, and when we give to others we somehow also receive. We see another surprising opposite when comparing these two verses in the Bible: 2 Corinthians 5:17 tells us: 'anyone who belongs to Christ has become a new person. The old life is gone; a new life has begun!' In contrast, James 3:2a says: 'we all make many mistakes.'

We might ask how these two statements can both be true at the same time – how can we make mistakes if we are God's new people? If God has made us new, why do we still sin from time to time, and as James says, in many ways?

Even the great Apostle Paul was still capable of sin and felt it very deeply when he let God down. He wrote about this in his letter to the Christians in Rome, but first went through some basics:

- all of us are cut off from God by our sin
- we cannot save ourselves by being good enough
- we all need a heart change
- our salvation is through faith in Christ
- the evidence that we are saved is in what we do
- when we are made right with God, he gives us peace, love and hope in our hearts and minds

Paul wrote what God has done for us in Romans 6:17-18: 'Thank God! Once you were slaves of sin, but now you wholeheartedly obey this teaching we have given you. Now you are free from your slavery to sin, and you have become slaves to righteous living.' The way we have been set free from sin is described in Romans 6:3: 'Or have you forgotten that when we were joined with Christ Jesus in baptism, we joined him in his death?' When we commit our lives to Jesus, we accept the death of our old nature and way of life that wanted to sin. Similarly, as Christ was raised to life again, we are also given a new life as God's Spirit makes our spirit alive.

The battle to obey God from our new nature rather than follow sin from our old nature is one that we all must fight. Paul said in Romans 7:24: 'Oh, what a miserable person I am! Who will free me from this life that is dominated by sin and death?' He felt that the old nature was like a dead body that he was always having to drag around with him. So, what is the solution? How do we overcome sin and live out of the new nature God has given us?

First, we can take encouragement that when we struggle, we are not condemned but still accepted by God. The fact that we struggle against sin is a sign of our new life! Romans 8:1-2 says: 'So now there is no condemnation for those who belong to Christ Jesus. And because you belong to him, the power of the life-giving Spirit has freed you from the power of sin that leads to death.' While it is true we are still capable of sin, there is a more powerful principle at work in our lives where God's Spirit helps us live a life that is pleasing to God. None of us will be perfect until Jesus returns, so we will still sin from time to time. Over time, however, he makes us more like Jesus.

Colossians 3:10 tells us: 'Put on your new nature and be renewed as you learn to know your Creator and become like him.' Every right choice we make as we walk with God will work out much better than sin. Here are some examples: spending time talking with God rather than screen time brings an experience of his peace and love; doing a thoughtful act to help another person is better than being selfish; having a gentle attitude toward others is better than causing conflict. Also, we will find that filling our minds with pure thoughts is better than wrong thoughts, and eating what is good for us leads to better health.

In your home, you might have various names and ages marked on a door frame. As humans, we grow in a fairly smooth pattern, with a growth spurt at puberty and then levelling off to our maximum height at adulthood. We might not notice we are growing from day to day, but if we look back at the marks on the door frame, we can see that growth has happened. Sometimes spiritual growth is steady, while at other times we realise we need God's help in a crisis, and we ask for the help of his Spirit as we surrender our lives more deeply to God.

The Apostle Paul in Galatians 5:22-23 says that the outcome of these choices is that: 'the Holy Spirit produces this kind of fruit in our lives: love, joy, peace, patience, kindness, goodness, faithfulness, gentleness, and self-control.' As we cooperate with God in making us more like Jesus, we grow in our relationship with God and know him more closely as our Heavenly Father.

Romans 8:13-15 says: 'But if through the power of the Spirit you put to death the deeds of your sinful nature, you will live. For all who are led by the Spirit of God are children of God. So you have not received a spirit that makes you fearful slaves. Instead, you received God's Spirit when he adopted you as his own children. Now we call him, "Abba, Father".'

So, it is the annoying opposite that we still have an old sinful nature to battle with while already being new people in Christ! The good news is that God has given us the power and encouragement of his Spirit to help us win the battle and grow in Jesus.

Further reading: Find the number of times the phrase 'even greater' is used in Romans 5; Hebrews 12:11

Why do we still do the wrong thing sometimes? (Week 33)

✏️ To answer

Match these words with their opposites:

kindness	hate
love	bossiness
sharing	selfishness
gentleness	grumpiness
patience	greed

💬 To discuss

1. Why do you think the Christian life seems to have so many opposites?

2. How might Romans 8:1 encourage you if you are feeling down?

3. Is there an area of your life where God wants you to become more like Jesus? How might you experience God's help to change?

▶️ To do

Find your old Plunket books or growth charts and look to see how much you have grown. Talk together about how you have also grown in Jesus.

🙏 Prayer

Our Heavenly Father and our God, thank you for giving me a new nature, even though it is sometimes hard to make right choices. Please help me remember to ask you for help at these times so that Jesus may be seen in my life. Amen.

Week 34

How do we grow in our relationship with God?

You may have heard the story in the Bible of Daniel in the lions' den and how God sent an angel to shut the lions' mouths and saved him. When the people of Israel were conquered by the King of Babylon, Daniel and his three friends, Shadrach, Meshach and Abednego, were taken as young people to Babylonia. Daniel refused to compromise his faith in God and so continued to pray and give thanks to God three times a day.

Because of their faithfulness, God was able to use Daniel and his friends to encourage the exiles and witness to his power to save them, even while they were doing an ordinary job working for the king.

As young people, my wife Linda and I were taught about having a daily devotional time. It was suggested that fifteen minutes each morning reading the Bible and praying was a good starting point. It wasn't given as a rule, but the devotional time was essential to grow our relationship with God. When we met together in various groups, we would often share what we had learned in our times with God. If we had missed having a devotional time that week, we were still encouraged by what others shared. I imagine Daniel and his friends would have talked about their faith in God together too.

Let's start with looking at the life of Jesus, as we always should when seeking any answers about life and faith. What was Jesus' education like, and how did he learn about his Father and the purpose of his life? How did Jesus develop his relationship with his Heavenly Father, and how did he maintain it through the trials of the three years of ministry and death on the Cross?

How do we grow in our relationship with God? (Week 34)

Children in Jesus' time received their first education from their parents, who were given the responsibility of teaching them God's ways, e.g., we read in Deuteronomy 6:7: 'Repeat them again and again to your children. Talk about them when you are at home and when you are on the road, when you are going to bed and when you are getting up.' This command was about everyday life, and parents were to provide a godly example and teach their children how to follow God.

Children in Jesus' time also attended a synagogue school, where they received an education in the first five books of the Old Testament. By age 12, a boy was considered qualified and called a 'son of the law'. There is a wonderful story in Luke 2:41–52 when Jesus went missing at age 12 following a family Passover trip to Jerusalem. He was found having a question-and-answer session with the teachers in the temple, where he amazed them with his answers.

Although it is helpful to spend time with God at specific times of the day, we don't want to forget him at other times. 1 Thessalonians 5:17 tells us to 'Never stop praying', so we should learn to pray and trust God in every part of life through the day.

How can we make a devotional time work out in practice?

First, pick a time of day that works for you, thinking of giving God your best.

Second, find a place where you are comfortable and can be undisturbed because time with God involves listening as well as praying.

Use a journal to write down what you learn. Make it regular so it becomes a habit, but if you miss a devotional time, don't beat yourself up.

When it comes to prayer, some people find the acronym ACTS useful to describe stages of prayer. This stands for:

Adoration. Praise God for his character and greatness, and tell him you love him. Be still in his presence and think about him.

Confession. This means to agree with what the Bible says about anything we have done that is sin. Ask him for forgiveness and for his Spirit's help to overcome temptation in the future. 1 John 1:9 promises us: 'If we confess our sins, he is faithful and just to forgive us our sins and to cleanse us from all unrighteousness.'

Thanksgiving. Thank God for the small, ordinary things as well as the larger things he has done for you.

Supplication. This is asking for the needs of others first, and then for our own needs. Pray for your family and friends to come to know Jesus.

Here is a suggested way to read the Bible during our devotional times.

Read it through

Pray before reading the Bible, asking for God's help to understand what you read. Expect God to speak to you about how he wants you to respond to him. Read the passage through a few times. A good way to start a Bible reading plan is in one of the gospels in the New Testament and in the book of Proverbs in the Old Testament. Many people have found the practice of memorising verses helpful too.

Dig it up

Ask yourself questions like: What is the main point of this passage? What does it teach about God or about me? Does it contain a promise or a warning?

Some people find it helpful to underline verses or to highlight their Bibles with various colours. One system that may work for you is a colour each for:

- The characteristics of God
- God's promises
- God's commands
- Questions we have

How do we grow in our relationship with God? (Week 34)

Pray it in

Pray about what you read and ask God to help you to live out what he has taught you.

Live it out

Remember during the day what God has spoken to you about in your devotional time and look for a way to put it into practice.

I also make a habit of praying and reading a passage of Scripture before going to sleep at night.

Further reading: Luke 2:41-52; Psalm 92:1-2; Psalm 55:17; Ecclesiastes 9:8

Growing in Jesus

✏️ To answer

Finish these sentences:

1. God is so great it makes us want to _____ .

2. If we tell God when we do wrong, he will _____ .

3. It is important to _____ God when he helps us.

4. It is helpful to ask God to help others _____ .

💬 To discuss

1. Someone once said: 'There is no substitute for time in God's presence.' What do you think of this statement?

2. How do you think God feels when you choose to spend time with him?

3. Try meditating on a passage of the Bible by reading it over slowly several times and asking God to speak to you. Some passages you could try reading are Psalm 37, John 1 or Proverbs 3.

▶️ To do

Put some milk (blue top works best) in a shallow dish with drops of food colouring around the outside. Each coloured drop could represent times during the day when we pray. Put a drop of detergent in the middle and watch what happens. Talk together about how God wants us to involve him in every part of life.

🙏 Prayer

Our Heavenly Father and our God, the example of Daniel and his friends is inspiring! Help us to spend time with you each day so we will be strong in faith when challenges come too. Through Jesus we pray. Amen.

Week 35

How do we become more like the Lord Jesus?

At our wedding reception, we had a three-tiered wedding cake. The top two layers were cut up and shared around our wedding guests. The bottom layer, following tradition, was carefully wrapped and stored away until the dedication of our first child, who was born three years later.

Now, I have a particular liking for fruit cake, and I must admit that several times during those three years, I suggested to my wife Linda that tradition might be put aside, and the cake sampled. You can imagine my disappointment to discover that when the day came to unwrap the cake, we found it had spoiled. Apparently, the best way to ensure a fruit cake will store well is to include a good quantity of cooking brandy in the recipe. Ours obviously didn't have enough.

There is a long word in the Bible that means both setting something aside and improving its quality. The word is 'sanctification'. It appears in the Old Testament when something or someone is set aside for a special purpose. For example, in Exodus 13:2, God instructed the people of Israel to set aside the first of their crops for him. At other times, they were told to sanctify God and give him first place in their hearts.

In the New Testament, the word sanctification has this meaning and one other. The first meaning is being separated from our old lives of sin to belong to God as holy. If we are Jesus' followers, we are already made holy in God's sight through Jesus' blood shed for us. Hebrews 13:12 describes this: 'So also Jesus suffered and died outside the city gates to make his people holy by means of his own blood.'

The second meaning of sanctification is the practical day-by-day process of being made more like Jesus, as Hebrews describes in chapter 12:14: 'Work at living in peace with everyone, and work at living a holy life, for those who are not holy will not see the Lord.' The word the Bible uses here for holiness is the same as the one used for sanctification. So, to summarise, through Jesus, we already belong to God, and we are still being made more like him. Both are sanctification.

In John 17:17-19, Jesus prayed this prayer for us: 'Make them holy by your truth; teach them your word, which is truth. Just as you sent me into the world, I am sending them into the world. And I give myself as a holy sacrifice for them so they can be made holy by your truth.' To be made holy in truth means to become like Jesus as he is Truth.

The Bible is the source of truth, and when we obey its teaching with the help of the Holy Spirit, we gradually become like Jesus. We also get to experience real and abundant life as a result. Romans 6:22 says: 'But now you are free from the power of sin and have become slaves of God. Now you do those things that lead to holiness and result in eternal life.'

2 Thessalonians 2:13 contains this promise: 'As for us, we can't help but thank God for you, dear brothers and sisters loved by the Lord. We are always thankful that God chose you to be among the first to experience salvation – a salvation that came through the Spirit who makes you holy and through your belief in the truth.' As Jesus is now in heaven, God's Spirit has been sent down to help us avoid sin and become more like Christ.

In Ephesians 3:14-16, we read Paul's prayer for the Ephesians: 'I fall to my knees and pray to the Father, the Creator of everything in heaven and on earth. I pray that from his glorious, unlimited resources he will empower you with inner strength through his Spirit.' This power includes practical wisdom in avoiding areas of temptation as well as the faith in God to strengthen us.

Recently, I bought a rusty, second-hand garden trolley. Before starting to use it, I had to spend some time scraping old flaking paint and rust off its metal frame and then painting it with a fresh coat of antirust paint. I'm keeping the leftover paint because I know that in a year or two, I will need to repeat the process on some parts of the trolley.

When we come to Christ, we are a bit like that rusty trolley. We are God's project, and he is delighted with us as we respond to his work in our lives and each day take on the image of his son a little more. Like I worked on the rusty trolley, God begins at first to change the more obvious things in our lives, swear words are taken from our conversation, we begin to use our money more wisely, and we become less selfish and more thoughtful of the needs of those around us. Gradually, our motives and attitudes also begin to change, and we start to dislike sin and love doing what is right.

Spending time with other believers also helps the process of sanctification. Jesus didn't die for a bunch of people who would stay as individuals but for the church, and he promises that together, we will be made perfect and glorify him. Ephesians 5:25b – 26 tells us: 'Christ loved the church. He gave up his life for her to make her holy and clean, washed by the cleansing of God's word.' As he works in our lives, God does something even better than I was able to do with my rusty trolley – he changes us from the inside out.

Further reading: Exodus 13:1-2; Joshua 3:5-6; 1 Corinthians 1:30; 1 Thessalonians 4:3-5

Growing in Jesus

✏️ To answer

Put these sentences in the right order:

God asks us to follow him.
God helps us to become more like Jesus.
We believe in the Lord Jesus and promise to follow him.
God's Spirit comes to live in our hearts.
We hear about Jesus.

💬 To discuss

1. What do you think or feel about being specially set apart to belong to God?

2. Which of the two meanings of sanctification means the most to you at present?

3. What is one practical step you might take to help you become more like Jesus?

▶️ To do

Do an experiment with ordinary, shiny nails. Try using water and salt to see what conditions make them rust the fastest. Try protecting the nails from rust using things like oil or wax. How does this rust you see compare to sin? Talk together about the practical steps we can take to avoid sin.

🙏 Prayer

Our Heavenly Father and our God, help us obey your call to give you first place in our lives. Thank you that you help us to grow in Jesus for your glory and our blessing. In his name. Amen.

Week 36

What does the Bible teach us about temptation?

I have a sweet tooth. While I was working at my desk yesterday, I remembered that in a jar in a cupboard were some sweets. After eating a couple of them (okay, to be honest it was more like half a dozen), I had to shift the jar to the other end of the house!

There are many areas in our lives where we can be tempted – small ones like sweets and larger issues like honesty and pride. Although the devil was defeated at the Cross, he continues to tempt us. 1 Peter 5:8-9a says: 'Stay alert! Watch out for your great enemy, the devil. He prowls around like a roaring lion, looking for someone to devour. Stand firm against him, and be strong in your faith.' We need not fear the devil because although he is more powerful than us, he is much less powerful than the Lord Jesus, who lives in our hearts.

At times, temptations can seem hard to resist, but the story of Job in Job 1-2 tells us that God places limits on how much Satan is allowed to tempt us. Not only that, but God has a good purpose in our lives behind the temptations he allows. He uses our trials to lead us, make us more like Jesus and glorify him. James 1:12 also tells us we will receive a crown of life in heaven.

Resisting temptation is about three main things:

- remembering God's Word,
- making wise choices to avoid situations where we will be tempted, and
- praying for God's strength to resist the temptation.

We read in Matthew 4:1: 'Jesus was led by the Spirit into the wilderness to be tempted there by the devil.' After praying and fasting for 40 days, Jesus was tempted in the same three main areas as we are – our physical desires, the desire to have 'things', and the desire for power and importance. Jesus resisted Satan's temptations because he had been praying and could answer each temptation with God's Word.

1 Corinthians 10:12-13 also gives us the promise of God's help, telling us that God puts limits on temptation and provides a way out. What is the 'way out' of temptation? It is our faith to believe God when he says he has a much better plan for us than to give in to temptation. For example, Matthew 5:6 tells us: 'God blesses those who hunger and thirst for justice, for they will be satisfied.'

Sin, like a diet of only sweets, never satisfies us but rather leaves us empty. Doing the right thing and obeying God, however, brings joy that no sinful pleasure can match.

In Genesis 39, Joseph was tempted by his master Potiphar's wife to sleep with her. Joseph had already thought through his response and pointed out the harm it would do to Potiphar and that it would be a great sin against God. In the end, Joseph's way of escape was to run out of the house! We all have weaknesses; maybe we are short-tempered, struggle with honesty or think too much about the opinions of our friends instead of what God thinks. If we follow the example of Joseph to think ahead about how to act, we can resist the temptation.

Jesus warned his disciples in Matthew 26:41 to pray: 'Keep watch and pray, so that you will not give in to temptation. For the spirit is willing, but the body is weak!' Pastor Charles Stanley used the acronym 'HALT' to help in the times when we are weak. It means to halt and pray when we are:

H ungry
A ngry
L onely
T ired

I have often found Philippians 2:13 a helpful verse. It says: 'For God is working in you, giving you the desire and the power to do what pleases him.' I have said to God many times: 'I don't feel like doing the right thing, but please help me do it', and God has answered that prayer. Psychologists tell us that to form a new habit takes on average 66 days. Each time we overcome a temptation, with God's help, it makes it a little easier next time until we are victorious over the temptation and get into the habit of doing good.

It is important to realise that being tempted is not the same as sinning. Don't let Satan make you feel guilty just because a thought has come into your head. But what if we do sin? Does that mean we are no longer Christians or that God will stop loving us? All of us are a work in progress, and God will restore us if we talk with him about the matter.

1 John 1:9 is a great reassurance: 'But if we confess our sins to him, he is faithful and just to forgive us our sins and to cleanse us from all wickedness.' The Apostle Peter, who denied Jesus three times at his trial and crucifixion, was wonderfully restored in his conversations with Jesus after the resurrection and went on to lead the church. Hebrews 4:15-16 is also a great encouragement: 'This High Priest of ours understands our weaknesses, for he faced all of the same testings we do, yet he did not sin. So let us come boldly to the throne of our gracious God. There we will receive his mercy, and we will find grace to help us when we need it most.' We can help one another by bearing one another's burdens also.

In everyday life we sometimes need to work out how the principles that the Bible teaches apply to specific situations. It's not always easy to see straightaway and requires grace for ourselves and others. But even though the Bible was written a long time ago, it still gives us a solid moral and ethical foundation that we can trust for our lives today. When we learn to obey the commands in the Bible for how to live in this world, we glorify God by trusting his Word. This also gives us the blessing of his peace and loving kindness in our hearts and lives.

Further reading: Proverbs 29:6; Job 1-2; James 3:2; 1 Timothy 1:15; Galatians 6:1-2; Matthew 4:1-4

Growing in Jesus

✏️ To answer

Finish this cloze by completing the words:

Being tempted is not the same as s_____. Wanting something another person has is not sin, but s_____ is sin. If we tell God about our sin, He will f_____ us and help us put it r_____ and give us p_____ in our hearts again.

💬 To discuss

1. Knowing that Jesus was tempted, how is being tempted different from sin?

2. How can good friends help us avoid sinning?

3. Is there a practical step you might take to keep away from places where you are tempted to do wrong?

▶️ To do

Have a family competition where each person takes a sweet like an Oddfellow or Mintie and puts it in their mouth. The winner is the person who can keep it in the mouth for the longest before it dissolves or is eaten. Talk together about the value of delayed gratification.

🙏 Prayer

Our Heavenly Father and our God, you know that we struggle with temptation sometimes. Please help us make right choices to stay close to you and to do good rather than give in to sin. In the strong name of Jesus we pray. Amen.

Week 37

What does it mean to be filled with God's Spirit?

In John 3, Jesus spoke to Nicodemus about being born again in the Spirit: 'The wind blows wherever it wants. Just as you can hear the wind but can't tell where it comes from or where it is going, so you can't explain how people are born of the Spirit.' Jesus was saying that there were things about God's Spirit that Nicodemus could not predict or understand.

In the Old Testament, there were only a few times when a person was anointed or given special power by God's Spirit. For example, Bezalel worked as a craftsman building the tabernacle, Othniel was filled with the Spirit for leadership, and others were anointed as prophets. At the time of the dedication of the tabernacle and later in 2 Chronicles 5:13b-14 with the temple in Jerusalem, the Holy Spirit showed the people that he was powerfully present by appearing as a pillar of fire or a cloud. By this, God was pointing to the future when his Son, Jesus, would die for humankind.

Later, before the birth of John the Baptist, his parents, Elizabeth and Zacharias were also filled with the Spirit, and in Matthew 3:16-17, God's Spirit came upon Jesus at his baptism to show us the pattern to follow. Jesus promised that the Holy Spirit would be sent to his followers after he returned to the Father.

John 14:16 tells us: 'And I will ask the Father, and he will give you another Advocate, who will never leave you.' This means the Holy Spirit's presence would no longer be limited to just a few people but would come to live in the hearts of all those who believed in Jesus. In this way, Jesus' presence can be simultaneously with all who believe in him.

In Acts 2, after Jesus went up to heaven, the disciples waited and prayed until the Holy Spirit was poured out, looking like tongues of fire on each person and sounding like a wind. Many people believed in Jesus and became his followers because of this, and miracles occurred. In the rest of the New Testament, this continued to happen as the gospel spread further.

What should we expect to be the result of the presence of the Holy Spirit in our lives? First, as Ephesians 1:13 tells us, the Spirit is present in our lives as proof of our salvation and to help us understand the Bible. As we read the Bible, God's Spirit helps us become more like Jesus. That is the most important part of being filled with the Spirit. Ephesians 5:18 tells us that the old nature that would like to sin is replaced by the character of Christ in us.

God also gives us the power of his Spirit to serve him, and we see many examples of this in the book of Acts. For example, in Acts 3:7-8, we read: 'Then Peter took the lame man by the right hand and helped him up. And as he did, the man's feet and ankles were instantly healed and strengthened. He jumped up, stood on his feet, and began to walk! Then, walking, leaping, and praising God, he went into the temple with them.' In Acts 5:15, we read that sick people were healed even when the Apostle Peter's shadow fell on them as he walked past.

In Hebrews 1:9, we read about Jesus: 'You love justice and hate evil. Therefore, O God, your God has anointed you, pouring out the oil of joy on you more than on anyone else.' Justice means right living, and the anointing of the Spirit on Jesus to perform miracles was because he lived a perfect life. God also wants to work in and through our lives, so it is important that we allow God to gradually develop Jesus' character in us so that he can use us in his service.

As we read earlier about Nicodemus, the experience of God's Spirit can go beyond our ability to explain it. So, what do we mean by the 'presence of God' in verses like Psalm 16:11 and Acts 3:19? First, we remember that God is omnipresent – he is everywhere. This means that even if we don't feel God's presence, he is still there, although sometimes, God does help us to feel his presence in a special way.

This can be, for example, to remind us of his holiness, give comfort and courage, help us worship him or renew our commitment to him. It can also be for guidance or to encourage us in prayer. God wants us to grow in a deeper relationship with him. Part of that will be, as Ephesians 4:30 and 1 Thessalonians 5:19 tells us, by not causing the Holy Spirit sorrow by how we live or ignoring his voice when he speaks to us.

As we surrender our lives to God and obey him in living the way Scripture teaches, we can expect that his Spirit will fill us. Ephesians 5:18 tells us to be filled with the Spirit and to give him praise and thanks from our hearts in song and prayer. We can also expect God to speak to us and give us power to help others.

An example of the Spirit filling believers with power is in Acts 4. Peter and John had been in prison, where they had been placed following the healing of the lame man we read about earlier. After they got out, they rejoined the church and prayed for God's power to continue to share the gospel. God answered, as we read in verse 31: 'And when they had prayed, the place in which they were gathered together was shaken, and they were all filled with the Holy Spirit and continued to speak the word of God with boldness.'

Further reading: Revelation 21:3; 1 Corinthians 2:12; 2 Corinthians 3:17-18; 2 Chronicles 5:13-14; Exodus 31:3 (Bezalel); Judges 3:10 (Othniel); Numbers 11:29 (Eldad and Medad)

Growing in Jesus

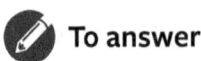 **To answer**

Read Acts 2:1-21 and put these parts of the story in the right order:

There was a loud wind.
People from other countries who were in Jerusalem could understand what was being said.
Peter stood up to speak and told them about Jesus.
Some people said the disciples were drunk.
Jesus' followers were all together in one place.
Flames appeared on all the disciples.
God's Spirit filled them, and they spoke praises to God in new languages.

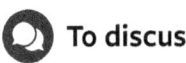 **To discuss**

1. Why does God choose to show his presence in a special way at times?

2. How can Ephesians 5:19-20 help us be aware of the presence of God through the day?

3. Jesus spoke of God's Spirit as the helper and as one who comes alongside us. Is there a need you have where you could stop and ask for his help?

 **To do**

Put half a teaspoon of baking soda in a square of tissue paper and twist it closed. Drop it into half a cup of vinegar. You may need to put the cup on a bowl or tray. Talk together about how this shows the action of the Holy Spirit in our lives.

 **Prayer**

*Our Heavenly Father and our God, thank you for the gift of your Spirit when I came to know you. Please fill me to overflowing with your life so that I might grow in you and have power to serve you.
Through Jesus I pray. Amen.*

Week 38

What does hope mean for a Christian?

Eighteen days after my now wife Linda and I started going out, I went on a five-week mission trip to a country in Asia. Linda and I were madly in love (we'd known each other for a year and a half) and knew we would get married.

A few days into the trip, while the team I was with was taking an evening church service, five fighters from a rebel Communist group, armed with automatic rifles, arrived to return an electronic device that had been stolen from one of our team members. They said they had killed the thief for us, and we were threatened with a similar fate if we spoke about supporting the government. They had also killed a pastor whom they suspected of informing on them a couple of weeks before we arrived.

We felt somewhat fearful, so we had a hasty team meeting about what to do. We agreed that we should stay on in the area and encourage the church, who were being faithful to God despite the danger they faced. You can guess what my main concern was – I wanted to get back home in one piece and marry Linda!

That night I said to God that I wouldn't stop praying until I knew we would be safe. After about two hours, this phrase from Psalm 91 burst into my mind: 'these evils will not touch you.' Deep down, I instantly knew that we would be okay; I fell asleep and slept like a baby.

The next morning, we were due to speak to the staff at a nearby plantation, but our team leader felt God was saying we should go somewhere else. At the time we would have been at the plantation, it was overrun by the Communist fighters and the staff were taken hostage. God's promise that we would be kept safe proved true throughout the trip.

Having hope is recognised as something that is important for our mental and emotional health. For most people, 'hope' means something we wish will happen but can't be sure of. 'I hope things will work out okay.' The focus of our hope can change suddenly and dramatically with a change in circumstances. A close friend can move away, a tragedy can occur in our family or ill health might come along.

For a Christian though, hope is something that we can be certain of and can base our life on. Hope brings peace, like the promise of safety that God gave me on that mission trip, but it goes further to give us security forever.

Psalm 71 is written by an older person, and we read in verse 5: 'O Lord, you alone are my hope. I've trusted you, O Lord, from childhood.' The writer's lifelong relationship with God has given them hope.

In Titus 3:4-7 we are told that hope comes if we are reborn through God's love and kindness to a relationship with him as his children. In Acts 23:6 we read that hope is associated with the resurrection of our bodies into the next life. Romans 5:1-5 describes that hope comes from what Jesus has done for us, making us right with God, bringing us peace in our hearts. Verse 5 reads: 'And this hope will not lead to disappointment. For we know how dearly God loves us, because he has given us the Holy Spirit to fill our hearts with his love.'

Although our hope is for salvation in the next life, and we aren't guaranteed an easy life here, we have hope in this life that God will give us his love, peace and strength to get through anything we face. God can give us a hope that nothing can put out.

We need to hold on to our hope in Jesus by faith, as Colossians 1:23 tells us, but we also have the wonderful promise that Jesus will hold on to us. In John 10:27-28, Jesus said: 'My sheep listen to my voice; I know them, and they follow me. I give them eternal life, and they will never perish. No one can snatch them away from me.'

In Colossians 1, Paul explained to his readers what God had done in sending Jesus. He said in verse 27: 'And this is the secret: Christ lives in you. This gives you assurance of sharing his glory.' 'Glory' means the shining presence of God in Jesus Christ, who is ruling in heaven and promises that all believers will one day be with him.

In the movie *The Knight's Tale* I love the speeches of Geoffrey Chaucer, who acts as the herald of Lord Ulrich of Gelderland. In one scene, Chaucer praises Ulrich to the crowd, finishing his speech with the phrase: 'we walk in the garden of his turpulence!' I didn't know what 'turpulence' meant, so I looked it up and found that it means: 'the feeling of being totally enveloped by another person's personality or presence'. I felt God's presence when he gave me his peace on the missions trip, but we are promised that in eternal life we will experience his glory fully.

Jesus invites us to have hope with these words in John 7:37-39a: 'Anyone who is thirsty may come to me! Anyone who believes in me may come and drink! For the Scriptures declare, "Rivers of living water will flow from his heart." When he said "living water," he was speaking of the Spirit, who would be given to everyone believing in him.'

Lastly, Paul's words in Romans 15:13 give us confident hope: 'I pray that God, the source of hope, will fill you completely with joy and peace because you trust in him. Then you will overflow with confident hope through the power of the Holy Spirit.'

Further reading: Psalm 39:7; Romans 12:12; Galatians 5:5

Growing in Jesus

✏️ To answer

Draw a picture of what you are hoping for.

💬 To discuss

1. How is hope in the Bible different from the way we talk about it in everyday life?

2. How might Jesus be wanting you to respond to his invitation to come to him and drink?

3. Does knowing that God invites you to experience his glory in the next life affect the way you live now?

▶️ To do

We can think of having hope as putting our hand into God's hand. Draw a large hand on a piece of paper or card and cut it out. Label it 'God's hand'. On each of the fingers write one thing that having hope in God gives to us.

🙏 Prayer

Our Heavenly Father and our God, thank you for giving us a definite hope in Jesus that helps us live for you in this life. Thank you for your promise that if we follow Jesus we will always be with you. In his name we pray. Amen.

Week 39

What does it mean when we say the Bible is inspired by the Holy Spirit?

Is the Bible more than just an ordinary book? Do we believe the words we read in it were inspired by God and are, therefore, words from God to us? It is important we answer these questions for ourselves, and if we believe them, then we need to decide if we will live by them, especially what they say about Jesus. Here are stories of two men who investigated the claim of the Bible to be inspired by God and found that it changed their lives.

Sir William Mitchell Ramsay (1851-1939) was a British archaeologist, New Testament scholar, and Professor at Oxford and Aberdeen Universities. Sir Ramsay was raised as an atheist and, at first, called the Bible 'a book of fables'. He travelled and explored Asia, where Paul the Apostle travelled on his missionary journeys, as recorded in Acts. Although he began his research work with the aim of disproving the Bible, what he discovered proved the opposite to be true. He later wrote: 'It was gradually borne in upon me that in various details the narrative showed marvellous truth.' His studies led him to be converted to faith in Christ.

J.B. Phillips (1906-1982) was an Anglican minister and Cambridge scholar who wrote the *New Testament in Modern English* by translating it from the original Greek. When he began his work, he viewed the New Testament as quite an ordinary book. When his translation was finished, however, he wrote the book *Ring of Truth: A Translator's Testimony*. He found the words he was reading were 'strangely alive' and that they affected him deeply. He realised that what he was reading couldn't have just been written by a human person, but that the Lord Jesus Christ was alive and speaking to him personally.

The phrase 'Ring of truth' was used to describe his confidence that the Bible was the inspired and living word of God.

To be confident in our faith in God, we need to have an authority outside of ourselves. The Bible is that authority, and it speaks to our hearts in a way that draws us into a relationship with God, showing us how to live. 2 Timothy 3:16 tells us: 'All Scripture is inspired by God and is useful to teach us what is true and to make us realise what is wrong in our lives. It corrects us when we are wrong and teaches us to do what is right.'

Also, 2 Peter 1:20-21 says: 'Above all, you must realise that no prophecy in Scripture ever came from the prophet's own understanding, or from human initiative. No, those prophets were moved by the Holy Spirit, and they spoke from God.' To say the Bible is inspired doesn't mean God took over the minds of the writers and made them robots. Rather, it means God spoke through them in a way that preserved their personalities.

As readers of the Bible, it is important to know how to read it, and theologians have developed guidelines for biblical interpretation to help us. If we have chosen to believe in and follow Jesus, we have received the Holy Spirit, and he gives us light as we read God's Word. 1 Corinthians 2:12 says: 'And we have received God's Spirit (not the world's spirit), so we can know the wonderful things God has freely given us.' The Bible contains teaching we can trust for this life and the next. It tells us of God's dealings with people from the start of creation, of our moral fall and of God's plan to redeem us back to himself again through Jesus.

As we read the Bible, we need to be careful not to add to what is written with extra rules or take away from it with human ideas. Nor should we ignore passages which make us uncomfortable. Most especially, we need to make sure that our understanding of Scripture always leads us closer to the Lord Jesus and honours him.

Deuteronomy 4:1-2 tells us: 'And now, Israel, listen carefully to these decrees and regulations that I am about to teach you. Obey them so that you may live, so you may enter and occupy the land that the Lord, the God of your ancestors, is giving you. Do not add to or subtract from these commands I am giving you. Just obey the commands of the Lord your God that I am giving you.' We can trust God that obeying what he teaches us through the Bible is always for our best.

Here are some pointers on how to read the Bible as God's Word to us:

- Think about what the author was intending to communicate. Often this is in the plain and direct reading of the passage.

- Read the verse in the context of the whole passage to get a better idea of the overall meaning of what God is saying.

- Read related passages in the Bible using cross references. A meaning that we take from a particular verse should always line up with the rest of the Bible.

- The passage could be written in a particular style (e.g. poetry, prophecy, instruction or wisdom). Each style needs to be interpreted slightly differently.

- We should read the Old Testament in the light of what Jesus did and taught (e.g. Jesus' teaching about the Sabbath in Mark 3:1-5).

- Understanding the culture of the time helps us to better understand how God wants us to relate to him (e.g. the place that idols had in people's hearts, and who the 'poor' were in society).

- There are some tiny inaccuracies and discrepancies in the Bible (e.g. the various gospel accounts of the number of angels at Jesus' empty tomb). J.B. Phillips says these are evidence of the 'ring of truth' of the Bible, because if the writers were making things up, they would have engineered their accounts to say exactly the same thing.

Further reading: Hebrews 4:12; Romans 15:4; 2 Peter 1:20-21

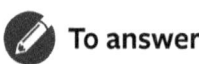 **To answer**

Challenge yourself to memorise the names of the books of the Bible or perhaps the New Testament to start with. What reward might you negotiate with your parents for doing this?

 **To discuss**

1. What do the words of 2 Timothy 3:16 mean to you?

2. Has a Bible verse spoken to your heart and mind recently? Might it encourage someone else too?

3. Are there parts of the Bible you have questions about? How can you find answers to those questions?

 **To do**

In New Testament times, it was usual for letters to be sealed shut with a blob of wax and an imprint of different colours using the personal seal of the person who wrote it. You might want to write a prayer to God and sign the prayer with a blob of wax with the letters of your name pressed into it while it is still soft. Search 'History of sealing wax' for more background. Talk together about the importance of trusting God even when we don't understand something.

Prayer

Our Heavenly Father and our God, thank you that we can trust the Bible to be your words to us. Please guide us as we read it so that we might grow to know you better and become more like the Lord Jesus. For your glory we pray. Amen.

Week 40

What does the Bible say about God's promises to us?

Can you remember sitting a test or handing in a project at school, then asking your teacher when you would get your grade back? If they promised a particular day, there have probably been times when you turned up to class only to hear it wasn't yet marked.

As a teacher, I can remember making promises about marking deadlines a number of times that I failed to keep – perhaps there was sickness in the family over the weekend, or perhaps I was just too optimistic about how long the marking would take. If we are honest, there will be promises we've made that we haven't kept too. You can probably see where this line of thought is going, so it won't be a surprise to hear that there is one person who has never failed to keep a promise!

The promises of God are given to us, but they come with three conditions. The first is that we trust completely what God is saying to us. One of the most wonderful stories in Scripture is that in Genesis 12-21 of Abraham and Sarah having their first child, Isaac, when they were very old. God had promised Abraham many years earlier that he would have a son who would be the first of very many descendants.

After many childless years and some wrong decisions on the part of Abraham and Sarah, it might have seemed to Abraham that it was a case of 'no son, no descendants'. Abraham, however, continued to believe God's promise despite the lack of evidence of Sarah becoming pregnant.

Although he made mistakes along the way, Romans 4:20-21 has this to say about Abraham's faith: 'Abraham never wavered in believing God's promise. In fact, his faith grew stronger, and in this he brought glory to God. He was fully convinced that God is able to do whatever he promises.' Over time, Abraham's faith grew through various experiences as he kept his life focused on living to glorify God.

Faith is like a muscle that gradually strengthens as we use it. Finally, when they were both quite old, Abraham's faith was ready to receive God's promise. Sarah became pregnant, and their son Isaac was born.

A second condition for receiving God's promises is that we are being obedient to him. In Hebrews 13:5b, we read this wonderful promise from God: 'I will never fail you. I will never abandon you.' If we are to experience the goodness of God's promises, however, there is a bit more to it. I hesitate to use an example about money because, in our culture, it is focused on too much, but let's look at the context of that verse.

Earlier in Hebrews 13, it also talks about giving hospitality to others (v2), caring for Christians in prison (v3), and, in the first part of verse 5, keeping our lives free from the love of money. The promises of God all have a condition of obedience we must meet to experience the blessing that comes with them. The idea in Hebrews 13 is that if we are good stewards of what God has given us and we put his kingdom first, then we can trust him to also meet our financial needs. This is not the same as earning God's blessings, though. Ephesians 2:8-9 tells us that all we receive from God is his free and undeserved gift to us. We obey him because he has put his love in our hearts.

A third condition of experiencing God's promises in our lives is patience. Some of God's promises are for each day, and others take some time to be fulfilled. Let's look at the difference. In 2 Peter 1:3-4, we read that God gives us promises for each day: 'By his divine power, God has given us everything we need for living a godly life. We have received all of this by coming to know him, the one who called us to himself by means of his marvellous glory and excellence. And because of his glory and excellence, he has given us great and precious promises. These are the promises that enable you to share his divine nature and escape the world's corruption caused by human desires.'

God will give us all the help we need each day to overcome sin and grow in Jesus – we only need to trust him and be obedient to his commands.

Sometimes, however, like Abraham, God gives us a personal promise for our lives in the future. Abraham had to wait 25 years from when God first spoke to him till when Isaac was born. Hebrews 6:15 tells us what Abraham did in the meantime: 'Then Abraham waited patiently, and he received what God had promised.' I wonder how much patience Abraham had at the start.

I am, by nature, quite an impatient person, and I can also think of promises in my life that took many years to be fulfilled. Why is that? James 1:4 says: 'But let patience have its perfect work, that you may be perfect and complete, lacking nothing.' (NKJV) As we continue to patiently trust God for his promises, we give him the opportunity to develop our character, teach us stickability and, above all, make us more like Jesus. That is worth far more than anything we might gain in this world!

Further reading: Here are some more of God's promises to us:
1 John 1:9 (Forgiveness); Isaiah 41:10 (God's presence with us);
John 16:33 (In Jesus, we have peace); Psalm 32:8 (Guidance);
Matthew 11:28 (Rest for our hearts and minds); Isaiah 40:31 (Strength);
Isaiah 9:6 (Our Father forever); Romans 15:13 (Hope for the future);
Isaiah 43:2 (Help in difficulties)

Growing in Jesus

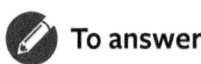 To answer

Try writing an acrostic poem using the word 'Promise'.

 To discuss

1. Why did God let it take so long for the promise he gave to Abraham to be fulfilled?

2. What is a promise from God (perhaps look at some of the verses in the 'Further reading') that is meaningful to you?

3. Which of faith, obedience or patience is the biggest challenge for you at present in receiving God's promises in your life? Pray and ask for God's help.

 To do

In Genesis 9:12-17, God promised with a rainbow never again to flood the earth. Fill a flat glass dish halfway with water and take it outside. Hold it above a white piece of paper on the ground. Slowly change the angle of the paper until a rainbow forms. If it is nighttime, you can turn the lights off inside and use a torch to shine down through the water instead. Talk together about a promise from God that has come true in your lives.

Prayer

Our Heavenly Father and our God, we thank you for your wonderful promises to always care for us. Please strengthen us to trust and obey you so we might receive your promises and bring glory to your name. Through Jesus we pray, Amen.

Week 41

What do the Ten Commandments teach us about our relationship with God?

To manufacture silicon chips for computers and phones, silica-based sand is used. Glass and metals, including gold, are then added in a very complicated process in a super-clean room. Before silicon chips were invented, computer information and music were stored on plastic tapes coated with magnetic iron oxide. You might see some of these old music tapes around your home.

After the people of Israel escaped from Egypt, God called Moses to go up Mount Sinai, where he gave him two flat stones on which were written the Ten Commandments. The Ten Commandments are a summary of the spiritual and moral laws the people had to follow. It's interesting to think about how God wrote the information on the stones and what kind of rock he used. Did the rocks contain some magnetic minerals? When we think about how information is now stored on chips made from ground-up rock, God was thousands of years ahead of us!

The Ten Commandments are just as relevant and important for us today as when God gave them to the people of Israel. We will look at each of the Ten Commandments over the next few weeks and see what they mean for us today. First, though, here's a bit of background.

The Ten Commandments were part of the covenant or special agreement God made with the people of Israel. This covenant was based on God choosing the people to belong to him and saving them from slavery in Egypt. In a similar way, God chooses us to belong to him even before we choose to follow Jesus.

When we believe, he saves us from the penalty of our sins and the hold sin has over us. God wants us to respond to his love by obeying his commandments and experiencing the wonderful freedom from sin and the harm it does. 1 John 5:3 tells us: 'For this is the love of God, that we keep his commandments. And his commandments are not burdensome.'

The first commandment is in Deuteronomy 5:6-7: 'I am the Lord your God, who rescued you from the land of Egypt, the place of your slavery. You must not have any other god but me.' The godhead, made up of the Father, the Son and the Holy Spirit, is one, is above all others, and is without fault. God wants to be number one in our hearts and for us to live lives that honour and glorify him. That doesn't mean, of course, that we don't love our family and others and that we can't enjoy hobbies and sports, but God wants to be first in our affections. As we make these choices to put him first, our lives gradually show his character, and we experience his peace and joy.

The word 'holiness' has a link with the word 'wholly', which has two meanings. First, we are to give ourselves first and completely to God, and then, as we become more like Jesus day by day, we become the whole people that God originally intended. James 4:8 describes this: 'Come close to God, and God will come close to you. Wash your hands, you sinners; purify your hearts, for your loyalty is divided between God and the world.'

Commandment two is Deuteronomy 5:8-9a: 'You must not make for yourself an idol of any kind, or an image of anything in the heavens or on the earth or in the sea. You must not bow down to them or worship them, for I, the Lord your God, am a jealous God.' It might seem strange to us in the West that people would make an image out of wood or metal and then worship and pray to it, but we also put our trust in things people have made. We can come to rely on electronic devices and possessions like cars and houses for financial and emotional security.

So really, an idol is anything that takes God's place in our hearts. A possession, hobby or sport that could be okay for one person and not affect their relationship with God could become an idol in another person's life.

This command not to have idols goes a bit further than just things. In this age, where so many people are image-conscious, we need to be different from the world. We cannot see God, but we can be reassured by faith that he is more real and lasting than the images and lifestyles we see portrayed in our culture. What is popular in the media will change next year, whereas the God we worship will last forever and always be fresh and new in our hearts.

The Apostle John gives us this advice in 1 John 5:20-21: 'And we know that the Son of God has come, and he has given us understanding so that we can know the true God. And now we live in fellowship with the true God because we live in fellowship with his Son, Jesus Christ. He is the only true God, and he is eternal life. Dear children, keep away from anything that might take God's place in your hearts.'

The third commandment is Deuteronomy 5:11: 'You must not misuse the name of the Lord your God. The Lord will not let you go unpunished if you misuse his name.' This means that we shouldn't use God's name as a swear word and that we should be sincere and not hypocritical when we talk about him. One memory that still grieves me is when I heard two students letting out a stream of bad language as they came out of class, where they had been praying a few minutes before.

If we are believers in Jesus, we bear his name, and so we need to ask him to help us so that our outside and inside lives match.

Further reading: 1 Samuel 2:2; Psalm 27:4; Psalm 63:1-8; Hosea 6:3; Psalm 115:4-8

To answer

Choose words from this list to fill the spaces in the questions.

Safe, idol, ten, first, none, name

1. An _ _ _ _ is something that we put before God.

2. God gave Moses _ _ _ commandments.

3. Commandment one says to put God _ _ _ _ _ in our lives.

4. Commandment three says not to use God's _ _ _ _ _ as a swear word.

5. God gave us the commandments to keep us _ _ _ _ .

To discuss

1. Why do the commandments that talk about our relationship with God come first on the list?

2. In what ways does obeying God's commandments protect us and make us free?

3. Are there any idols in our lives – things that we think of first before him that we need to surrender to God?

To do

Find some clean, flat stones and paint a favourite Bible verse or picture on one. It will help to undercoat the stone first. Fine brushes and acrylic paints are best, and a layer of clear coat at the end can make it look good too. Talk together about the verses you have chosen.

 **Prayer**

Our Heavenly Father and our God, we trust that your commandments are given to keep us safe from the harmful effects of sin. Please help us to obey you and keep you first in our lives. We want to grow to know and love Jesus, who has done so much for us. Amen.

Week 42

How do the Ten Commandments help us to get along well with each other? Part 1

In this next section of commandments, we start getting into the 'You shall nots.' People who don't know God sometimes say that he is a kill-joy, meaning they think he wants to take away our enjoyment of life. Nothing could be less true. The commands were given not against people but against sin, which is our enemy as well as God's. The laws God gave through Moses were also fairer and morally and ethically higher than in other countries near Israel.

Commandment four is in Deuteronomy 5:12-14a,15: 'Observe the Sabbath day by keeping it holy, as the Lord your God has commanded you. You have six days each week for your ordinary work, but the seventh day is a Sabbath day of rest dedicated to the Lord your God. Remember that you were once slaves in Egypt, but the Lord your God brought you out with his strong hand and powerful arm. That is why the Lord your God has commanded you to rest on the Sabbath day.'

The benefit of obeying this command is to have the physical, mental and emotional rest we need from learning and work. In Mark 2, Jesus' disciples were criticised for picking heads of grain to eat on the Sabbath when they were hungry. Jesus defended them in verses 27-28 by saying: 'Then Jesus said to them, "The Sabbath was made to meet the needs of people, and not people to meet the requirements of the Sabbath. So the Son of Man is Lord, even over the Sabbath!"' God has not made us just to work but also to take rest and have recreation.

It is also important as we rest that we remember our relationship with God. We can think about all of God's goodness to us in creation and thank

God for what he has done for us. Jesus often took time out to be with his Father by going to places where he wouldn't be disturbed to pray. In most churches, the Sabbath means Sunday, but we shouldn't leave resting and being refreshed just to that day. Taking time out when we need to be refreshed spiritually, as well as in other ways, is essential.

Let's look at the fifth commandment. Deuteronomy 5:16 says: 'Honour (respect, obey, care for) your father and your mother, as the Lord your God has commanded you, so that your days [on the earth] may be prolonged and so that it may go well with you in the land which the Lord your God gives you.' (Amplified Bible)

Soon after our first child was born, I realised that having children brought a much bigger challenge to put aside my selfish desires than getting married did. Whatever the newborn's needs were (and it was sometimes hard to figure just what was needed!), they had to be met regardless of whatever else we wanted to do at the time. Babies can't do anything for their parents, so for quite a while, the relationship is all give without any expectation of receiving back. As children grow up, that gradually changes, and at some point in later life, if parents are ill, the roles of giving and receiving may flip around the other way.

So, respecting our parents means recognising and showing gratitude for all they have done for us and caring for them if needed.

Obeying our parents is sometimes a hard one! If our parents are genuinely caring for us, there shouldn't be a problem, except in cases where we have faith in God, and they are opposing that. Otherwise, it is important to recognise that they have been on the earth a lot longer than us and have accumulated a store of experience and wisdom that can be trusted to be for our best. Obedience can sometimes be hard, especially through our teenage years if our parents haven't started to gradually allow us more freedom and responsibility. God promises, though, to be with us and to help us if things are difficult.

Deuteronomy 5:17 says: 'You must not murder.' This looks like an easy commandment to keep, but in Matthew 5:21-26, Jesus extended this to doing violence to another person – including with our words. Proverbs 18:21 says: 'The tongue can bring death or life; those who love to talk will reap the consequences.' Usually, our mouth gets us in trouble by saying too much rather than too little! Our words can wound others deeply.

More positively, our words can also do a great deal of good if what we say builds others up and encourages them. Barnabas, who accompanied Paul on his first missionary journeys in the book of Acts, was known as the 'son of encouragement'. His example and that of Jesus are good ones to follow!

Commandment seven is in Deuteronomy 5:18 and says: 'You must not commit adultery.' Adultery refers to a wrong relationship with someone you are not married to, or a wrong relationship before marriage too. Marriage, as God planned in the first part of Genesis before Adam and Eve sinned, is the foundation of family life and contributes to a healthy society.

Similarly to the last commandment, 'You shall not murder', Jesus also took this commandment against adultery further. In Matthew 5:27-28, he said that if someone looks at another with wrong thoughts, then they are as guilty of breaking this command as if a physical act had taken place. Of course, we are not responsible for thoughts that come into our minds as temptations, but we are responsible if we think further on them rather than replacing them with godly thoughts and helpful Scriptures.

Further reading: Proverbs 7:6-23; Exodus 20:11; Luke 2:51

How do the Ten Commandments help us... Part 1 (Week 42)

 **To answer**

Join up the opposites in these lists:

rest	encourage
disobey	marriage
murder	respect
adultery	work
keeping God's laws	harm

 To discuss

1. What are the benefits of respecting our parents?

2. What ways can you think of where the Sabbath commandment about having rest helps us?

3. Is there anyone we have angry feelings toward that we need to put right with God?

 To do

Scientists who study rocks have found in them information about magnetic fields from the past – a little like the information in old computer and music tapes. There are a lot of fun experiments you can do with a magnet. Use a U-shaped magnet to test various objects and see if they are magnetic. If you are in a place with rocks containing iron, you might like to try those too. Think about questions like: Are all metals attracted to the magnet? How far away from the magnet can it attract things? Try dragging an object around on cardboard with the magnet on the other side.

Talk together about what attracts you to God.

| 203

Growing in Jesus

 **Prayer**

Our Heavenly Father and our God, thank you for our parents and for those who help us learn more about your love. When we are tempted to do wrong toward others, please give us wisdom and strength to keep obeying you, knowing you always want the best for us. Help us to keep growing in Jesus, we pray. Amen.

Week 43

How do the Ten Commandments help us to get along well with each other? Part 2

We carry on this week with commandment eight in Deuteronomy 5:19: 'You must not steal.'

In Acts 19, we read about the Apostle Paul teaching about Jesus in the city of Ephesus, near modern-day Turkey. In Ephesus, there was a temple dedicated to the worship of the goddess Artemis. Silver coins and other objects with her image made up an important part of the trade.

It's interesting to read Paul's instruction to the young Ephesian church in Ephesians 4:28: 'If you are a thief, quit stealing. Instead, use your hands for good hard work, and then give generously to others in need.' Perhaps some of those new believers had previously made a living by stealing valuable silver items, the results of the efforts of others. Either way, they were now to earn an honest income by working and looking out for the needs of others.

Theft can happen in other ways. John 10:10 tells us that theft is a part of the character of Satan, our enemy. If you have ever had something stolen, you know how it feels to lose something precious that you had worked to buy. Leviticus 6:2-5 tells us that theft can mean failing to return something we have borrowed or through dishonest or unjust financial dealings.

Something that is legal is not always ethical or fair. Romans 13:7 tells us that we should pay our share of taxes to the government. Not only that, but we are also reminded to 'give respect and honour to those who are in authority.' Theft doesn't have to be just money or possessions; we can steal from someone when we dishonestly take credit for what they have done, e.g., copying answers in a test.

This leads us to commandment nine, in Deuteronomy 5:20: 'You must not testify falsely against your neighbour.' Proverbs 12:22 also tells us: 'The Lord detests lying lips, but he delights in those who tell the truth.' This command not to lie also includes exaggerating. Have you looked at photos of people holding up fish they caught and noticed if the fish is held out at arms' length toward the camera, it makes it look larger? More seriously, though, it is worth taking a few moments to check ourselves on what we say. If no one is around to correct what we are saying, it is easy to stretch the truth.

Work hard to get a reputation for integrity and honesty. James 4:6 tells us that God gives us extra grace if we struggle to keep commands like this if we come to him in honest prayer and ask him for help.

There is one area where both stealing and lying can be involved, and that is gossip. Gossip means passing on something we have heard to another person when they are neither part of the solution nor part of the problem. It can be tempting to try to seem important by gossiping about what we have heard or seen. We need to remember that whatever we know will only be part of the picture – there are always two sides to any coin. Rather, when we have information about a person, our attitude should always be to love them as our neighbour by seeking their best and we usually do that by keeping quiet or helping if we can. Gossip is a way of stealing from someone's reputation, and if we pass on gossip that isn't true or is exaggerated, we are guilty of lying.

Finally, commandment ten in Deuteronomy 5:21 reads: 'You must not covet your neighbour's wife. You must not covet your neighbour's house or land, male or female servant, ox or donkey, or anything else that belongs to your neighbour.' Covetousness means a strong desire to have things just because someone else has them.

At present, one of the richest people in the world is the Frenchman

Bernard Arnault, with over $200 billion. He owns a huge company that makes luxury fashion goods, jewellery, champagne and yachts. If there was ever a list of things anyone would want, he probably has all of them! Yet, Jesus said in Matthew 6:19-21: 'Don't store up treasures here on earth, where moths eat them and rust destroys them, and where thieves break in and steal. Store your treasures in heaven, where moths and rust cannot destroy, and thieves do not break in and steal. Wherever your treasure is, there the desires of your heart will also be.'

Why did Jesus say that? No matter how much we have, fallen human nature will always want more wealth, even if it is just to store it up somewhere it can't be used for good.

King Solomon was the richest and most powerful ruler in Israel's history, but partway through his rule, he started disobeying some commands God had given him. He carried out great building projects, spent money on luxury possessions, married more wives who didn't follow God and so on. Toward the end of his life, he wrote the book of Ecclesiastes, describing how he never found happiness in these things after all.

In Ecclesiastes 6:9, Solomon wrote: 'What the eyes see is better than what the soul desires. This too is futility and striving after wind.' Striving after wind means something that can never be caught or found. Solomon recognised too late that what Jesus said in Matthew 6 makes perfect sense – that desires in our souls or hearts can never be met outside of an obedient relationship with God.

Instead of wanting everything others have, we should focus on growing in our relationship with God and serving him. This will bring God glory and along the way give us satisfaction and contentment that lasts forever.

Further reading: 1 Timothy 6:6-10; 2 Corinthians 8:21; Ephesians 4:25; 1 Corinthians 6:10

Growing in Jesus

✏️ To answer

Mark these as true (T) or false (F):

Lying is sometimes okay.

Riches can make people happy.

We can rest on days other than Sunday.

Words don't hurt people.

We only have to obey our parents when they are watching us.

💬 To discuss

1. How does trusting God help us not want what others have?

2. How can we act for the good of others (and ourselves!) if people are starting to gossip about them?

3. What should we do if we have cheated in a test?

▶️ To do

You know that solid steel objects will sink in water, right? It is possible, though, to float a steel sewing needle on the surface tension of water. Put the needle on a piece of tissue paper on top of water, and as the tissue paper soaks up water, it should sink, but leave the needle floating on top. Make sure the water is kept completely still, though. See which way it points – it should point north to south like a magnetic rock. Talk together about the signposts God gives us to guide our lives.

 Prayer

Our Heavenly Father and our God, thank you for your wisdom in giving these commandments to help us all live together happily. We pray for courage and strength to obey them and to put right anything that we have done wrong. We ask this for your glory and through Jesus our Lord and friend. Amen.

Week 44

What does holy communion mean?

About the same time that I became a Christian, a friend also came to faith. Geoff had been used to going to a few parties where most people drank beer and sometimes too much of it. When he came to faith, he stopped drinking and wanted to show his friends that his life had changed, so though he still went to the parties, he took a bottle of milk to drink instead. It was quite a conversation starter!

Until he rose from the dead, the last time Jesus ate with his disciples was just before his crucifixion, when they celebrated the Jewish festival of Passover together. Passover started just before the people of Israel were preparing to flee from Egypt to the land God had promised them. In Exodus 12, God told them to use a lamb without fault as the main part of the meal and to put some of its blood on the doorway of their house in the shape of a cross. This Passover festival would also mark the start of the year for them as a way of remembering how God had rescued them.

As Jesus ate the last Passover meal with his disciples before his crucifixion, he used the wine and bread they were sharing to explain how they represented his blood and body, which would soon be given for them as he died on the Cross. Jesus also said his blood would bring about a new covenant for those who trusted him for forgiveness of their sins.

A covenant is an agreement or treaty between two parties. The new covenant Jesus announced, and under which we live, is between God and everyone who puts their faith and trust in Jesus. On God's part, he promises to forgive us through the blood of Jesus that was shed and place his Spirit in our hearts, so we can fellowship with him. It also means we get to share in the inheritance of Christ.

Just as a human treaty often needs a go-between to bring two peoples together, so Jesus giving his body to die on the Cross bridges the gap between us and God. Our part of the new covenant is to place our trust fully in the Lord Jesus and obediently follow him.

Most churches today celebrate communion together – it can have various names like the Eucharist or the Lord's Supper. As we share symbols like grape juice and bread, we obey Jesus' command to remember him, as we read in 1 Corinthians 11:23-25: 'For I pass on to you what I received from the Lord himself. On the night when he was betrayed, the Lord Jesus took some bread and gave thanks to God for it. Then he broke it in pieces and said, "This is my body, which is given for you. Do this in remembrance of me." In the same way, he took the cup of wine after supper, saying, "This cup is the new covenant between God and his people – an agreement confirmed with my blood. Do this in remembrance of me as often as you drink it."'

As we discussed earlier, Passover marked the beginning of the year for the people of Israel. In a similar way, as we share in communion together, we are remembering that our faith in Jesus' sacrifice of his body and blood is the beginning of our new life.

In New Testament times, the early churches usually celebrated communion as they gathered on the first day of the week. They often got together for celebration meals as a practical way of expressing their love to one another. Jude 12 and other places speak of these gatherings as 'fellowship meals', and they often happened in people's homes. The name 'fellowship meals' was perhaps because they shared food together as a way of looking out for the needs of others who were less fortunate. These times were also for teaching and prayer and probably to share communion, as we read, for example, in Acts 20:7 of the church at Troas.

Communion on the first day of the week reminds us to put Jesus first regularly in our lives, and the symbols of his body and blood remind us of what he paid for us to bring forgiveness and new life. When we take communion, it is also important to consider Paul's words to the Corinthians in 1 Corinthians 11:28-29: 'That is why you should examine yourself before eating the bread and drinking the cup. For if you eat the bread or drink the cup without honouring the body of Christ, you are eating and drinking God's judgement upon yourself.'

Communion is a time to search our hearts and minds and confess and turn from any sins we have not made right with God. In particular, as the Corinthian church included both rich and poor, it was a chance for the richer members to honour the poorer ones by putting their needs first in their shared meals.

Today, we can ask ourselves if we are seeking to be good neighbours to others and if we are obeying Jesus' command to love one another as he loved us. By doing this, we are at least in part honouring Jesus' words to us in John 15:13-14: 'There is no greater love than to lay down one's life for one's friends. You are my friends if you do what I command.'

Further reading: Acts 20:7; Genesis 9:11-17; Genesis 17:1-8

What does holy communion mean? (Week 44)

✏️ To answer

Number these sentences from the Last Supper in the right order.

Jesus shared bread with his disciples.
The disciples found the room that Jesus had told them about.
Judas lied about betraying Jesus.
Jesus shared wine with his disciples.
Jesus said one of the disciples would betray him.

💬 To discuss

1. What is our part of the new covenant that God has made with Jesus' followers?

2. How does communion remind you of what God has done for you?

3. How can celebrating communion help to keep us close to the Lord Jesus?

▶️ To do

Think about when the early church gathered for fellowship meals. Talk together about someone you can bless with a meal. Could you take extra food to school to share at lunchtime?

🙏 Prayer

Our Heavenly Father and our God, we are amazed that you love us enough that you were willing to give your Son to die for us. Please help us to remember to love you first and follow you in all parts of our lives. Through Jesus we pray. Amen.

Week 45

What is baptism about?

Before Jesus started his ministry, he went down to the Jordan River, where John the Baptist was baptising people. They were coming because of John's message to repent and put their lives right with God. John had spoken to the crowd to tell them that someone was coming who was a much better person than him, and that in the future, that person would baptise people with the power of the Holy Spirit.

When Jesus asked John to baptise him, John argued, saying that it was he who should be baptised by Jesus. Jesus insisted, saying in Matthew 3:15: '"It should be done, for we must carry out all that God requires." So John agreed to baptise him.' Although he was sinless and didn't need to repent, by being baptised Jesus was showing us two things.

First, he was commissioned and given power by the Holy Spirit to preach about the Kingdom of Heaven and to heal and bring people freedom from demonic forces. This was confirmed, as we read in the next two verses in Matthew 3:16-17: 'After his baptism, as Jesus came up out of the water, the heavens were opened, and he saw the Spirit of God descending like a dove and settling on him. And a voice from heaven said, "This is my dearly loved Son, who brings me great joy."'

Secondly, just as God had saved the people of Israel hundreds of years before by miraculously leading them through the Red Sea and the Jordan River, Jesus was showing everyone God's plan that, through him, God would bring the world the offer of salvation from sin. Although Jesus knew his ministry would end in his death, by being baptised he was showing his willingness to be obedient. Jesus said later in John 8:29: 'And the one who sent me is with me – he has not deserted me. For I always do what pleases him.' Jesus delighted to do his Father's will out of love, even though he knew it would cost him so much.

After Jesus rose to heaven three years later, the disciples carried on preaching this good news about Jesus. It was normal then for new believers to be baptised as a sign that they were leaving their old lives behind. In his first sermon, Peter said to the hearers in Jerusalem on the day of Pentecost in Acts 2:38: 'Each of you must repent of your sins and turn to God and be baptised in the name of Jesus Christ for the forgiveness of your sins. Then you will receive the gift of the Holy Spirit.'

Later, the gospel spread to Samaria, a land near Israel, and then further still to the Gentiles or non-Jews. The pattern was still for all those who believed to be baptised and to receive the Holy Spirit.

Let's look more at what baptism means. In Romans 6:4, Paul wrote: 'For we died and were buried with Christ by baptism. And just as Christ was raised from the dead by the glorious power of the Father, now we also may live new lives.' So, we can think of baptism as symbolising a death and burial that takes place as we go underwater, followed by a new life as we come out of the water again.

When our church in Wellington was meeting at a school, several of us had to go in early one Sunday morning to fill up a portable pool for a baptism service. The school headmaster walked past while we were working and suggested we leave an empty beer bottle in the pool to stand for the old life the person would be leaving behind!

Depending on what our life has been like before we came to know the Lord Jesus, we can think of various things we might want to leave behind. It doesn't mean we will never sin again, of course, but it does mark a point where we have repented and said that we belong to God from here on.

The great apostle and leader Paul said in 1 Corinthians 15:31b: 'I face death daily.' As well as physical danger, the Christian walk was one of every day remembering the promise he made to God when he believed and was baptised. We die to sin and our selfish desires and seek to live a life out of wholehearted love for God and our neighbours.

Reading on in Romans 6:5, we read the promise God gives us when we obey him and place our faith in Jesus in baptism: 'Since we have been united with him in his death, we will also be raised to life as he was.' The same powerful Holy Spirit who raised Jesus from the dead will also raise our physical bodies to life again one day to be with God forever. Today, as we seek to serve him, we rely on the power of the Holy Spirit to do through our lives what we cannot do by ourselves. If Jesus looked to the Holy Spirit to empower his ministry, so we must also.

Baptism is also a public acknowledgement that we now belong to God. As we make that commitment publicly, it strengthens our faith. In most cases in the New Testament, people were baptised in a public setting, and apart from some countries nowadays where to do so is dangerous, this is still usually the case.

In Matthew 10:32-33, Jesus said: 'Everyone who acknowledges me publicly here on earth, I will also acknowledge before my Father in heaven. But everyone who denies me here on earth, I will also deny before my Father in heaven.' This means that when we are baptised, we can be reassured that Jesus stands with us.

Further reading: Colossians 2:12-15; Exodus 14:13-22; Acts 2:38

What is baptism about? (Week 45)

 To answer

Complete this cloze by finishing off the words in the spaces:

Baptism means the e _ _ of our o _ _ life and the start of a new o _ _ .

It means we b _ _ _ _ _ to G _ _ now.

 To discuss

1. How does Jesus' baptism show us an example to follow in our lives?

2. In which areas of your life can you ask God for power from his Holy Spirit?

3. What might you leave behind in a baptismal pool if you were baptised?

 To do

Read Acts 16:23-34. Act out the arrest of Paul and Silas and how God delivered them and saved the jailer and his family.

Characters: Paul, Silas, jailer, other prisoners, jailer's family.
Props: prison doors, chains, water.
Clothing: robes, headwear, sandals.

Talk together about what this teaches you about how powerfully God works.

Prayer

Our Heavenly Father and our God, thank you for giving us a model in the life of Jesus to follow. Please give us courage to leave behind the things that are wrong and to be ready to tell that we belong to you. Through Jesus we pray. Amen.

Week 46

How does the Lord carry our burdens?

Halfway through my last year at high school and shortly before I became a Christian, I changed my course from commerce to sciences. That meant that six months later, when I began study at university, I was about a year and a half behind and facing a huge challenge to catch up. In addition, I had committed to a scholarship to teach while fearing speaking in front of more than two or three people at once! My high school principal had tried to talk me out of changing my course, but I was grateful that he had finally allowed me to move to sciences.

In many ways, in that first year, I felt out of my depth, and Paul's words in 2 Corinthians 12 meant a great deal to me. The Apostle Paul had been struggling with his own weaknesses – he had an ongoing health problem, and he wasn't a good speaker. He also suffered from opposition and criticism, even from some of his friends.

Paul did the best thing he could do and took his problems to God in prayer. In 2 Corinthians 12:9-10, Paul wrote this to describe God's answer: 'Each time he said, "My grace is all you need. My power works best in weakness." So now I am glad to boast about my weaknesses, so that the power of Christ can work through me. That's why I take pleasure in my weaknesses, and in the insults, hardships, persecutions, and troubles that I suffer for Christ. For when I am weak, then I am strong.'

Paul was a person of opposites. He had opposed Christians to the point of being involved in putting some to death, but was then called by God as an apostle to spread the message of Jesus. The answer Paul received from God also contained opposites. To get strength from God, he needed first to accept and talk to God about his weaknesses. While he felt weak, God would give him the strength he needed to serve him.

I found the same principle true in my first year at university. I trusted God and studied hard, and even though my marks were low to start with, at the end of the year I found I had passed everything.

There is an old saying, 'Where God guides, he provides.' If we are walking in God's will, there is no challenge he puts before us that we can't learn to overcome in his strength. There will be times we feel it too much for us, but God will always give us his strength as we ask for his help. Another wonderful passage that can encourage us is Isaiah 40:30-31: 'Even youths will become weak and tired, and young men will fall in exhaustion. But those who trust in the Lord will find new strength. They will soar high on wings like eagles. They will run and not grow weary. They will walk and not faint.' The idea in this verse is that in exchange for giving God our weaknesses, he will give us his strength.

Once we have learned this, God will also help us learn to trust him in what we are good at. Sometimes that happens when we experience failure. Paul was highly educated, a deep thinker and strong leader. When he listed all these qualifications in Philippians 3, however, even the things he was good at he said he counted as loss. This was so he might be close to God and know God's power at work through his life.

Two things can get in the way of us knowing God deeply and fulfilling his plan to serve him: what we think we can't do (our weaknesses) and what we think we can do (our self-confidence). Both need to be handed over to God in exchange for his life in us. After I overcame my fear of public speaking, I found it was something God had made me good at. I must still remember to rely on him each time I speak, however, so that his words, and not just mine, can bless those who hear.

Jesus gave a wonderful illustration of how he wants us to depend on him. In John 15, he says that he is a vine and we are like the branches, connected to the life of the vine and bearing fruit for him. Our part is not to look at our weaknesses nor be proud by depending on ourselves, but to stay connected to him as our source of life.

Here is what Jesus says in John 15:4-5: 'Remain in me, and I will remain in you. For a branch cannot produce fruit if it is severed from the vine, and you cannot be fruitful unless you remain in me. Yes, I am the vine; you are the branches. Those who remain in me, and I in them, will produce much fruit. For apart from me you can do nothing.'

Notice what Jesus says – that without relying on him, we can do absolutely nothing. Of course, we know we can go off and do any number of different things without thinking about God. That, however, is not how God has planned us to live. The Bible tells us that in the end, whatever we do apart from him won't glorify him or bless others. Instead, he wants us to live a life of obedience to his commands and trust in his strength through each day.

Further reading: 2 Corinthians 1:8-10; 1 Peter 5:7; Matthew 11:28-30

How does the Lord carry our burdens? (Week 46)

✏️ To answer

Use the words from this list to complete the sentences below.

obedient, stay, vine, talking, branch

Jesus said he is like a _____ and we are the _____. He wants us to _____ joined to him. We can do that by reading the Bible, being _____ and _____ to him.

💬 To discuss

1. How does being honest about our weaknesses mean God can help us?

2. Are there talents or gifts in your life that God wants to give you strength to use?

3. Is there a worry you are having that you can give to God and leave with him (Philippians 4:6)?

▶️ To do

Just as life flows from a vine into its branches, so God has also put life into seeds. Put some small seeds, like mustard seeds (which you might have in the kitchen cupboard), between two layers of damp paper towels and try to grow them.

Talk together about how we can experience God's life and help.

🙏 Prayer

Our Heavenly Father and our God, thank you that when we feel we are weak we can ask you for strength. We praise you that you always stick by us, even when we face challenges. Please guide us and strengthen us to grow in Jesus day by day, we pray. Amen.

Week 47

How are we to pray?

Most of us are familiar with the 'Lord's Prayer' in Matthew 6, which is often prayed in church. This week, we will look at what Jesus taught about prayer a little earlier in Matthew 6.

Jesus had been correcting the religious leaders, who gave money publicly to show off to others how generous they were. Jesus then gave the same teaching about prayer in Matthew 6:5-8: 'When you pray, don't be like the hypocrites who love to pray publicly on street corners and in the synagogues where everyone can see them. I tell you the truth, that is all the reward they will ever get. But when you pray, go away by yourself, shut the door behind you, and pray to your Father in private. Then your Father, who sees everything, will reward you.'

Jesus teaches us some wonderful things about prayer in these verses. First, while it is good to pray with others, e.g., in a youth group, it is important that we remember who we are praying to and to have an attitude of humility. The hypocritical religious leaders whom Jesus was talking about had forgotten that; and as a result, their prayers were not answered. Instead of praying to be heard by others, Jesus said that we should do the opposite and find the most private place we can to pray. The wonderful thing is that when we pray alone, we find our Heavenly Father is already there waiting for us and will reward us.

No matter how old we are, we also need to pray with the simplicity of faith and trust of a child. When the disciples tried to stop people bringing their children to Jesus for a blessing, he said in Mark 10:14: 'Let the children come to me. Don't stop them! For the Kingdom of God belongs to those who are like these children.' Children instinctively trust their parents for everything they need. God wants us to have the same simple faith in him.

Secondly, when you pray to God by yourself, it is the two of you together. God is present in every place at the same time, so when you pray to him, you are the object of his complete love. We don't need to worry that God will only listen to us for the first minute or two, then go offline and be unavailable. As long as we aren't trying to cover up sin in our lives, we can talk to God about anything and everything. We can have peace that he will answer all our requests according to what he knows is best for us.

So, what can we talk to God about? As he is a perfect father, we can ask for strength or wisdom about any situation or decision we might face. We can ask him for direction, to meet a need, or for his help to carry a burden we have in our hearts. If you had a father to talk to when you were little, perhaps you thought he knew everything. As you grew older, you realised he didn't know everything and wasn't perfect after all. God, as our Heavenly Father, is all powerful and knows everything. He is perfect and never changes.

Some days, going into our room and praying feels like the last thing we want to do. I have often felt like that, but afterwards, I am glad I took the time to pray. Talking things over with God and being in his presence lightens our load and brings a sense of joy and peace. That is what Jesus meant when he said: 'Your Father who sees in secret will reward you.'

Lastly, Jesus said in this passage: 'Your Father knows exactly what you need even before you ask him!' Sometimes when we ask God whether we should do something, he gives us a definite 'yes' or 'no', but often he helps us to understand 'how' something should be done – meaning with right attitudes and motives. Through learning 'how', God changes us to become more like Jesus while we pray.

How do we find out what God knows we need? Prayer is about more than speaking to God. It is also about listening and being willing to obey him no matter what answer he gives. As well as talking to God, we need to learn to be quiet and listen in prayer. To know that what I believe God is saying to me is actually his voice (and not the effect of last night's double cheese pizza!), I always have my Bible open. God will never say anything different to what he has given in his Word.

In the next chapter in Matthew, Jesus taught about persistence in prayer. Matthew 7:7-11 says: 'Keep on asking, and you will receive what you ask for. Keep on seeking, and you will find. Keep on knocking, and the door will be opened to you. For everyone who asks, receives. Everyone who seeks, finds. And to everyone who knocks, the door will be opened. You parents – if your children ask for a loaf of bread, do you give them a stone instead? Or if they ask for a fish, do you give them a snake? Of course not! So if you sinful people know how to give good gifts to your children, how much more will your Heavenly Father give good gifts to those who ask him.'

It is wonderfully encouraging to know God wants us to come to him in prayer and to answer our prayers for his glory and our best.

Further reading: Philippians 4:6-7; Mark 11:24; Luke 18:1-8

How are we to pray? (Week 47)

To answer

Find the five words in this Word Find that God promises us as we pray.

V	G	I	F	T	S
I	O	Q	W	N	O
C	O	H	E	A	R
B	D	T	K	J	Y
Z	S	H	E	L	P
A	N	S	W	E	R

To discuss

1. God already knows what we need, so why do we still need to pray?

2. Is there a verse or passage from the Bible that has been especially meaningful to you? Can you talk to God about how he wants it to work out in your life?

3. Do you need to spend more time with God in prayer?

To do

Google 'String can telephone, Scientific American'. Make a string telephone and try it out. Talk together about how God hears us when we pray, even if we can't see him.

Growing in Jesus

 **Prayer**

Our Heavenly Father and our God, it is so wonderful that even though you are in heaven and we are on earth, we can talk with you through prayer. Help us remember you are with us in every moment of the day and that you are strong enough to answer any prayer. Through Jesus we pray. Amen.

How are we to pray? (Week 47)

✏️ To answer

Find the five words in this Word Find that God promises us as we pray.

V	G	I	F	T	S
I	O	Q	W	N	O
C	O	H	E	A	R
B	D	T	K	J	Y
Z	S	H	E	L	P
A	N	S	W	E	R

💬 To discuss

1. God already knows what we need, so why do we still need to pray?

2. Is there a verse or passage from the Bible that has been especially meaningful to you? Can you talk to God about how he wants it to work out in your life?

3. Do you need to spend more time with God in prayer?

▶️ To do

Google 'String can telephone, Scientific American'. Make a string telephone and try it out. Talk together about how God hears us when we pray, even if we can't see him.

| 225

Growing in Jesus

 **Prayer**

Our Heavenly Father and our God, it is so wonderful that even though you are in heaven and we are on earth, we can talk with you through prayer. Help us remember you are with us in every moment of the day and that you are strong enough to answer any prayer. Through Jesus we pray. Amen.

Week 48

What does worship mean?

Have you ever noticed that when you've looked at photos of dogs and their owners, they sometimes look alike? More seriously, there is truth in the saying that we become like that which we focus on. In other words, we become like that which we worship. If we love money, we can become greedy. If we focus on our own pleasure, we will become careless about things that count for the next life. If we focus on worshipping God, however, we will gradually become more like Jesus.

What comes into your mind when you hear the word 'worship'? For most of us, worship probably brings to mind a church service once a week. This makes sense because we want to praise God. But is worship just what we do for an hour, one day a week? What about the other days?

In the Old Testament, the people of Israel were commanded to bring sacrifices to worship God, first in the tabernacle, and then later in the temple in Jerusalem. To worship God required cost and effort in those days. They had to select the first of their crops or their animals, and then make a long journey uphill to the temple and back. For our worship of God to be meaningful, it should also cost us something as we learn to focus on God before our own needs and wants.

In the Samaritan woman's conversation with Jesus in John 4, she asked him where God should be worshipped. Jesus said it soon wouldn't matter where God was worshipped, but: 'The time is coming – indeed it's here now – when true worshippers will worship the Father in spirit and in truth.' It was the coming of Jesus into the world and his death on the Cross that changed how and where worship happened.

Jesus taught that what mattered most was giving God first place in our hearts. Revelation 21:3b says: 'God's home is now among his people! He will live with them, and they will be his people.' God comes, by his Holy Spirit, into the heart of every person who believes in Jesus and chooses to follow him, and so worship happens from our hearts, in all places and at any time.

Philippians 3:3 says God is pleased when we realise we 'put no confidence in human effort', meaning that in all situations, we should trust God's wisdom first. In that way, all parts of our lives become worship to God.

Secondly, we thank God for the gift of his Son and all that means – for forgiveness and being able to have a relationship with him. We thank him for the fellowship of his Spirit, for his written Word, for prayer and all his goodness to us. We also praise him for his constant love, mercy and faithfulness, his power as Creator, his wisdom, holiness and glory.

In the Bible, the word 'worship' also contains the idea of service to God. Colossians 3:17 says: 'And whatever you do or say, do it as a representative of the Lord Jesus, giving thanks through him to God the Father.' This means that in every area of life – our family life, our schoolwork, friendships, hobbies and sports, we should make what we say and do an offering of worship to God. We do this by giving Jesus first place in our lives, obeying his commands and loving others.

Romans 12:1-2 also talks about making worship a part of our daily lives: 'And so, dear brothers and sisters, I plead with you to give your bodies to God because of all he has done for you. Let them be a living and holy sacrifice – the kind he will find acceptable. This is truly the way to worship him. Don't copy the behaviour and customs of this world, but let God transform you into a new person by changing the way you think. Then you will learn to know God's will for you, which is good and pleasing and perfect.' Worship involves gradually being changed from the inside out.

In Matthew 15:8, Jesus spoke of people who seemed to worship God but whose way of living was far from him. As we draw near to God each day, we may become aware of sins we need to confess. In Hebrews 10:19-22 we read: 'And so, dear brothers and sisters, we can boldly enter heaven's Most Holy Place because of the blood of Jesus. By his death, Jesus opened a new and life-giving way through the curtain into the Most Holy Place. And since we have a great High Priest who rules over God's house, let us go right into the presence of God with sincere hearts, fully trusting him. For our guilty consciences have been sprinkled with Christ's blood to make us clean, and our bodies have been washed with pure water.'

True worship is when our inward and outward lives match up.

As we gradually learn to do that, we find that our experience of God's love grows, leading to us growing in our love relationship with him. This will make us glad to serve him in whatever he asks us to do.

Further reading: Psalm 2:11; Psalm 66:1-4; Revelation 4

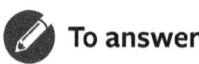 **To answer**

Revelation 4 describes worship happening in heaven. Read the chapter and draw a picture of something you have read there.

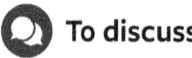 **To discuss**

1. What does a 'living sacrifice' mean in Romans 12:1?

2. What does it mean for you to know that God wants to have a two-way loving relationship with you?

3. Is there an area of your thinking that God would want to renew?

 **To do**

Have a family time of worship together – put on some worship music and experience God's presence as you worship God. The New Zealand artist Steve Apirana has a great rendition of the song 'Living Sacrifice'. Talk together about what you can praise God for.

 **Prayer**

Our Heavenly Father and our God, thank you for the privilege of being able to worship in public. Please help us to follow you in all parts of our lives in throughout the week. We praise and thank you that you are worthy of all our worship. Through Jesus we pray. Amen.

Week 49

How does God want us to give to help others?

One summer, while I was on a break from university, our church had a speaker discussing the needs of a medical mission in Haiti. I sensed God was speaking to me to give my last week's pay from my factory job, which had just finished, and I did so. It was a few weeks before university lectures started again. Soon after, a friend working in a wool store suggested I speak to his foreman there, and as a result, I managed to get work for a couple more weeks before university resumed.

Jesus said in Luke 6:38: 'Give, and you will receive. Your gift will return to you in full – pressed down, shaken together to make room for more, running over, and poured into your lap. The amount you give will determine the amount you get back.' The blessing for me wasn't the money from the two-week job but in learning to be generous and seeing God meet my needs.

God's nature is to be generous, and we see this above all in his giving his life for us. As we learn to give, we become more like him, which leads to much greater and lasting blessings than mere money. It is still important to learn to handle money in a biblical way, however, and it can be one of the more difficult areas to get right in life.

In 2 Corinthians 8:5, Paul commended the believers in Corinth who had responded to his appeal for funds to support Christians in Judea. These distant believers were experiencing famine at the time. Paul commended the Corinthian church because they gave themselves first to God in worship and to the needs of their suffering brothers and sisters. Our attitude should be the same, and as Jesus taught in Matthew 6:3, we should give in secret as much as possible.

Jesus laid down tough challenges to people who wanted to follow him when he saw that the love of riches was getting in the way of their commitment to him. In Luke 16:13, Jesus said: 'No one can serve two masters. For you will hate one and love the other; you will be devoted to one and despise the other. You cannot serve God and be enslaved to money.'

Part of the reason why Judas Iscariot betrayed Jesus was his love for money, which showed up in his dishonesty with the money he looked after for the twelve disciples. Ecclesiastes 5:10 says: 'Those who love money will never have enough. How meaningless to think that wealth brings true happiness!' God warns us that no matter how much we have, it will never satisfy our inner needs – only Jesus can do that!

In contrast to seeking wealth in this world, in Matthew 6:20, Jesus instructed us to gradually store up treasure in heaven where it will last forever.

One way to store up treasure is by being generous as God makes us aware of needs he enables to meet. The Christian life can be viewed like a pool with water flowing in and out, so it remains fresh. If the outlet becomes blocked up, however, and water only flows in, the pool will eventually become stagnant, without much life.

In Acts 20:35, Paul said to the Ephesian church: 'And I have been a constant example of how you can help those in need by working hard. You should remember the words of the Lord Jesus: "It is more blessed to give than to receive."' In this verse and similar passages, Paul makes it clear that working diligently is a character attribute that God wants us to have. We are not to be lazy. Gaining money is a good thing if it is earned honestly, because it can be a blessing to many people.

Two of the Christian leaders I most admire are Billy Graham, the American evangelist, and John Wesley, the eighteenth-century English founder of Methodism. Early in their ministries, both chose to receive just a moderate level of income. They kept to this commitment by living carefully and giving the rest away to Christian ministries, including the needs of the poor. John Wesley said, 'Gain all you can, save all you can, give all you can'. By setting a moderate and sensible level of income, both men avoided the temptations of wealth.

Proverbs 30:8b-10 puts it like this: 'Give me neither poverty nor riches! Give me just enough to satisfy my needs. For if I grow rich, I may deny you and say, "Who is the Lord?" And if I am too poor, I may steal and thus insult God's holy name.' If we look at what others around us have and feel bad that we don't have what they do, it is worth considering how what we do have measures up with the rest of the world. Taking the average household income in New Zealand for the average-sized family, a global wealth calculator puts us approximately in the top 7 percent in the world!

Lastly, John Wesley said this about the good that money can do: '(Money) is an excellent gift of God, answering the noblest ends. In the hands of his children, it is food for the hungry, drink for the thirsty, raiment (clothes) for the naked. It gives to the traveller and the stranger where to lay his head. By it we may supply the place of a husband to the widow, and of a father for the fatherless; we may be a defence for the oppressed, a means of health to the sick, of ease to them that are in pain. It may be as eyes to the blind, as feet to the lame; yea, a lifter up from the gates of death.'

Further reading: Mark 6:8; Acts 20:33-35; 1 Timothy 6:6-10

 **To answer**

Read the story in James 4:13-17 and make up a different ending.

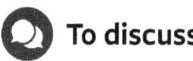 **To discuss**

1. Is having money 'evil'? Why or why not?

2. How do you think the Corinthian Christians felt when they sent money to the Judean Christians for famine relief?

3. Is there something from John Wesley's beliefs about money that you could make part of your life?

 **To do**

Play a game like Monopoly but introduce an extra rule where a player can give money or points to help another player. Talk together about how this extra rule might guide us in using money in real life.

 **Prayer**

Our Heavenly Father and our God, thank you for what you have given us. Please give us wisdom with money and possessions, so our hearts stay true to you. Help us honour you and grow in our Lord Jesus, we pray. Amen.

Week 50

What did God do at Christmas?

Can you remember your first Christmas? My earliest memory was getting a wind-up Hornby train set running on metal tracks. I was quite young because I can remember putting coal in the funnel and not understanding why smoke didn't come out.

My toy train ran in just two dimensions, around and around on a flat track – no ups or downs. Try to imagine your life was like that, so that everything that happened to you was on a perfectly flat surface, like a train track with no height or depth. If we lived in two dimensions, we wouldn't be aware of anything above or below us. As we went through our daily lives, everything would be like stick figure drawings on paper.

It is the start of the four-week Advent season as I am writing this. At home and church, we are reading all the Bible passages that prophesied about the coming of Jesus into the world, about the appearances of angels, Mary and Joseph, the shepherds and the wise men. Along with these characters, who we often see in Christmas plays, there were also two other people, both of whom were looking to heaven for the person God was sending into the world. One of these people was an old man named Simeon.

On the day Joseph and Mary took the baby Jesus to the temple to dedicate him as their firstborn to God, Simeon was sent by the Holy Spirit to meet them there. This is what happened, as recorded in Luke 2:28-32: 'Simeon was there. He took the child in his arms and praised God, saying, "Sovereign Lord, now let your servant die in peace, as you have promised. I have seen your salvation, which you have prepared for all people. He is a light to reveal God to the nations, and he is the glory of your people Israel!"'

Simeon was a righteous man and was closely in touch with God through prayer. He knew God had promised to send a Saviour into the world who would rescue his people from sin. When he saw Jesus, Simeon recognised him as the answer to the promise in Isaiah 9:2: 'The people who walk in darkness will see a great light. For those who live in a land of deep darkness, a light will shine.'

When we come to know and follow Jesus, a light is turned on inside us, and our spirit comes alive. As a result, we can sense a new dimension we haven't seen before. It is like we have lived our lives on a flat, two-dimensional train track, and now we can see above and below. It is like we were living as stick figures, and now we are real people. We have been made alive through a relationship with God through Jesus. For me, my first Christmas as a Christian was the most meaningful because I now had a relationship with God.

What else is in the Christmas story? If we go back a couple of chapters in Isaiah, we read these words in Isaiah 7:14: 'All right then, the Lord himself will give you the sign. Look! The virgin will conceive a child! She will give birth to a son and will call him Immanuel (which means "God is with us").' We understand already that when Jesus was born to Mary, God entered the world as fully human to fully reveal himself to us and to die so we might be saved from sin.

When we read this verse in context, however, we find a richer meaning. The prophecy in Isaiah 7:14 was given as part of a message that Isaiah took to Ahaz, the king of Judah. Ahaz was being threatened by an attack from two other kings and by the powerful nation of Assyria. God told Ahaz to ask for a sign as deep or as high as he wanted to show his trust in God to deliver him. Instead, Ahaz refused to trust God by asking for a sign and went his own way, apart from God.

Many people are like King Ahaz and don't want to put their faith in God, preferring to trust in their own wisdom and efforts in life. When we believe in the miraculous birth of Jesus and trust him as our Saviour, we show our trust in God. As we experience 'Immanuel, God with us' in all parts of our lives, we grow in our relationship with him. What are the ways in which God wants to show us that he is with us?

Let's look at Isaiah 9 and see what God promises in the Lord Jesus and what it means.

Isaiah 9:6 reads: 'For a child is born to us, a son is given to us. The government will rest on his shoulders. And he will be called: Wonderful Counsellor, Mighty God, Everlasting Father, Prince of Peace.'

- 'The government' means God has authority over everything that concerns us as we trust him.
- 'Wonderful Counsellor' means God has sent the Holy Spirit and his Word to advise us on the best way to live.
- 'Mighty God' means God has more power than anyone or anything else.
- 'Everlasting Father' means God promises he will always be a Father to us.
- 'Prince of Peace' means we have peace with God when we are forgiven, and we can also rest in peace in Jesus no matter what is going on in the world around us.

Further reading: Luke 2:1-21

Growing in Jesus

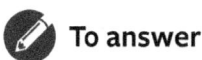 **To answer**

Unjumble these five Christmas words.

GELAN   AYMR   ABBY   PEESH   SSJEU

 To discuss

1. In what ways could it mean that Jesus is the light of the world?

2. Which one of the descriptions of Jesus in Isaiah 9:6 is most meaningful to you?

3. What does Christmas mean to you if you have trusted your life to Jesus? If you haven't taken that step, how might Christmas be different for you?

 To do

Set out or make Christmas tree decorations that tell some of the Christmas story. Talk together about what Christmas means to each of you.

 Prayer

Our Heavenly Father and our God, thank you for the gift of your Son into the world and that he is alive now for us to follow. Because of your immeasurable love, we give you all of our hearts and lives in return. Through Jesus we pray. Amen.

Week 51

What does it mean to have God as our Father?

The term 'Father' is only used about 15 times to describe God's relationship with his people, Israel, in the Old Testament. One example is in Deuteronomy 32:6, where Moses told the people of Israel, whom God had saved by miraculously rescuing from Egypt: 'Is this the way you repay the Lord, you foolish and senseless people? Isn't he your Father who created you? Has he not made you and established you?' God wanted the people of Israel to experience him as their Father, but they had difficulty believing.

In the New Testament, Jesus referred to God as his Father over 150 times, and many other passages refer to us as God's children. For example, in John 1:12, we read that all who receive Jesus as Lord and Saviour are given the right to become children of God. Jesus said he and the Father were one, so when we know the Lord Jesus, we also have a relationship with our Heavenly Father.

Galatians 4:4-6 talks about God as our Father too: 'But when the right time came, God sent his Son, born of a woman, subject to the law. God sent him to buy freedom for us who were slaves to the law, so that he could adopt us as his very own children. And because we are his children, God has sent the Spirit of his Son into our hearts, prompting us to call out, "Abba, Father".'

In this passage, we see all three members of the Godhead mentioned. The Son pays the price for us to be redeemed or bought back for God, then God the Father sends his Spirit into our hearts to help us understand and experience that he is now our Father. The term 'Abba Father' refers to us not just as young dependent children but also as those who have grown up but who still need a relationship with their father to get ongoing advice and support. It is perhaps a little like a father-and-son/daughter business, where the adult children are apprenticed to their father and learn from and work alongside him daily.

As a father, I have always tried to show God's character and love to my children, but I know that I haven't always got it right! None of us have had perfect fathers and not all of us have been privileged to have a good relationship with our earthly fathers. My father was 20 years older than my mother and suffered poor health, so he played little part in our lives. I missed out on a lot of wisdom and advice as a result. For some of us, the relationship with our fathers has even been negative.

God is very different from that and wants to be closely involved in our lives. We might think we don't deserve to be in his family and are just second-class daughters or sons. God, however, adopts us by grace as we read above in Galatians 4, to make us fully his children with complete rights to his protection and love. Adoption by God isn't a kind of 'Plan B'. God has planned from the very beginning that we would be his children. We were in his thoughts before we were born.

The Bible also mentions that God's care for us is like that of a concerned and caring mother. Isaiah 49:15-16 says: 'Never! Can a mother forget her nursing child? Can she feel no love for the child she has borne? But even if that were possible, I would not forget you! See, I have written your name on the palms of my hands.'

In Luke 13:34, Jesus expresses the same sentiment when he describes his wish to gather the people of Jerusalem to himself like a mother hen with her chickens.

Finally, God guarantees us a wonderful inheritance with the Lord Jesus. Our inheritance as believers starts from the moment we receive new life. What is included in our inheritance?

- We inherit a place in the Kingdom of God (Matthew 25:34). This includes a particular calling to serve God, and the gifts to carry it out.
- We inherit salvation (Hebrews 1:14) and eternal life (John 3:16).
- We inherit a blessing (1 Peter 3:9) and the promise of future glory (Romans 8:17-18), living eternally with him.

Jesus said in John 14:2-3 that he has gone to prepare a place for us. 1 Corinthians 2:9-10a gives us a glimpse of that future life: 'That is what the Scriptures mean when they say, "No eye has seen, no ear has heard, and no mind has imagined what God has prepared for those who love him." But it was to us that God revealed these things by his Spirit.'

How do we get to know our loving Heavenly Father now? In John 5:19-20, Jesus said he did what he saw his Father doing. Perhaps, in a similar way that Jesus learned to be a carpenter by watching Joseph, Jesus copied his Heavenly Father and did what he showed him.

God has given us all worthwhile work to do, and we learn to know him better as our Father as we serve him. This happens as we build a relationship with him in reading the Bible and praying, then learning how to show our love for him in being obedient to him. A wonderful part of the blessing of experiencing God as our Father is seeing what he will do through our lives as we serve him in the plan he has for us.

Further reading: Matthew 6:9; John 10:30; Psalm 103:13-14

Growing in Jesus

 **To answer**

Use the first letter of the words in the spaces to complete the cloze:

God gives us a place in his k _____ . He gives us enjoyable j _____ to do and e _____ life. God b _____ us and has a special place for us to l _____ in heaven.

 **To discuss**

1. Why do you think Jesus referred to God as his Father so many times?

2. What does the illustration of a hen with its chickens tell us about God's care for us?

3. What does it mean for you to share an inheritance with Jesus?

 **To do**

Have someone take a turn being the father in your family, perhaps for an evening or one afternoon in the weekend. What would you have to think about or do? Talk together about how each of you learned from this experience.

 **Prayer**

Our Heavenly Father and our God, thank you for being the very best Father we could imagine. Help us to grow as your trusting children so we might bring glory to you. Thank you for the Lord Jesus, who calls us his brothers and sisters. In his name we pray. Amen.

Week 52

How do I set a good foundation for my life?

Several years ago, friends of ours bought a house in a fairly new subdivision. It was a lovely modern home, but after a couple of years, they needed more space, so decided to extend it. After having plans drawn up, they started digging the foundation, expecting to hit rock soon. Unfortunately, it was about seven metres down before they found solid ground.

They discovered the subdivision had been developed on the site of an old rubbish tip, which was then covered with soil. Eventually, they finished the extension and later moved overseas. New owners moved in, but several years later, the house exploded and was destroyed – fortunately with no injury to the family! Rubbish tips contain a lot of organic matter, which when it breaks down, produces flammable methane gas, which had built up under the house.

This story reminds us that we need to build a good foundation for our lives and that things are not always what they seem. You may have read the story Jesus told in Luke 6:46-49 of the two builders: 'So why do you keep calling me "Lord, Lord!" when you don't do what I say? I will show you what it's like when someone comes to me, listens to my teaching, and then follows it. It is like a person building a house who digs deep and lays the foundation on solid rock. When the floodwaters rise and break against that house, it stands firm because it is well-built. But anyone who hears and doesn't obey is like a person who builds a house right on the ground, without a foundation. When the floods sweep down against that house, it will collapse into a heap of ruins.'

When we watch buildings going up, it always seems to take longer than expected before the 'up' part starts to happen. The higher the building is planned to go, the deeper and stronger the foundation must be.

In Jesus' story, the house on the sand probably went up faster and cost less because it had no foundation. That builder was probably able to have a housewarming party a long time before the other builder and had left-over money to spend on food and drink for his friends. The first builder was wiser, however, because after the storm had come through, his house remained standing. His friends would have praised him for the extra work he had done earlier.

What does this story tell us about how we build our lives? The first thing is that the rock foundation of the house represents the Lord Jesus. People choose to base their lives on many different ideas and goals, but basing our lives on Jesus and what he taught is the only way that is solid, true and leads to life. Only Jesus can cleanse us from our sins, change us from the inside out, and promise us a future with him after this life. 1 Corinthians 3:11 tells us: 'For no one can lay any foundation other than the one we already have – Jesus Christ.' Whether we will follow him or not is the most important choice of our lives.

Second, we must be patient and have faith in God to build a good foundation. This means building a relationship with him by reading the Bible, praying and obeying its teaching. Foundations take time. Good attitudes, good habits and character also take time to develop as none of us learn good life lessons first time, every time!

Thirdly, as well as deciding on the foundation, we can also decide what price we will pay for the materials we use to build with. 1 Corinthians 3:12 tells us we can choose to build on the foundation with gold, silver, jewels, wood, hay or straw. The difference between these is what they cost and how long they last.

To follow Jesus, obey him and experience all he has for us will cost us. It will cost us pride as we learn to humbly obey and become unselfish. Sometimes it will also cost us pain when we must leave sin behind as we let God change us. It may also cost us misunderstanding from others.

Lastly, there will be a time when our work is tested. Every building that goes up must be inspected to make sure it complies with building rules meant for our safety. At the end of our lives or on the day Jesus returns, what we have built in our lives will be tested. In 1 Corinthians 3:13, we are told: 'But on the judgement day, fire will reveal what kind of work each builder has done. The fire will show if a person's work has any value.' Obviously, gold, silver and diamonds cannot be destroyed by fire, but wood and straw will be burned up.

2 Peter 1:5-7 gives us some final advice about building our lives: 'In view of all this, make every effort to respond to God's promises. Supplement your faith with a generous provision of moral excellence, and moral excellence with knowledge, and knowledge with self-control, and self-control with patient endurance, and patient endurance with godliness, and godliness with brotherly affection, and brotherly affection with love for everyone.'

This passage reminds us of Jesus' words in Luke 6:46-47. The wise person is the one who takes time to grow a relationship with God, listening to learn his ways and then obeying him one step at a time.

Further reading: 2 Peter 1:5-7; Hebrews 12:1-2

Growing in Jesus

✏️ To answer

Put each of these words into one of the two lists below:

foundation, obeys, deep, ruined, fell, disobeys

House on sand	House on rock

💬 To discuss

1. What is God's part in building in our lives and what is our part?

2. Which building materials in 2 Peter 1:5-7 do I want to have in my life at present? What might that look like in practice?

3. Is there a good habit we want to learn? How can God help us with that?

▶️ To do

Use dominoes or Jenga blocks to build two towers as high as possible. Build one on a hard floor like lino and the other one on a soft surface like a fluffy rug. Talk together about what the results taught you about Jesus' story of the two builders.

🙏 Prayer

Our Heavenly Father and our God, please give us the courage and patience to build a good foundation in our lives as we grow in the Lord Jesus. Give us wisdom to make good choices and to always base our lives on your Word and your way. We thank you for all your promises in Jesus. Amen.

 **About the author:** Barry Jackson is a first-generation Christian of 50 years and a graduate of Faith Bible College. He has been a secondary teacher and educational leader in state and Christian schools both in New Zealand and overseas. He and his wife Linda have two children and two grandchildren.

www.ingramcontent.com/pod-product-compliance
Lightning Source LLC
Chambersburg PA
CBHW051209290426
44109CB00021B/2393